The
HUSBAND'S
Manual

Cherrydale Books
Sun Star Press
Arlington, Virginia

Printed and bound in the United States of America. First printing 1996.

ISBN: 0-96322336-4-5

LCCN HQ756.M813 1996
646.7'8—dc20   95-51466
CIP

Bookstores: For bulk rates, write to Cherrydale Books, P.O. Box 10329, Arlington, VA
22210

Lyrics on p. 20 reprinted by permission of the songwriters, Stephen Longfellow Fiske
and Jai Joseph.

Table of Contents

Why This Book?

Many men are used to working with manuals—car manuals, home repair manuals, income tax manuals, etc.

This book is similar: It's a how-to. Step-by-step, easy-to-read directions for being the best husband you can be and making things work in your marriage.

The Husband's Manual is written for the guy who wants to do the right thing and will do what it takes to have the best marriage possible.

Chapter 1 lays the groundwork: Three rules about the husband's role and how he can lift his marriage above the ordinary.

Chapters 2-50: Practical ways to apply the three rules in daily life.

• • •

At his wedding a husband usually senses that he is embarking on a challenging and exciting journey. Sometimes he loses track of that sense in the crush of everyday affairs. But the simple events of everyday life can be the building blocks for those original feelings and dreams. Much of this book is a reminder of the basics, how not to forget them, and how important they are in contributing to a marriage that remains an unending adventure.

Preface

We take life as a joy and a challenge.

When we were planning to be married, we spent a lot of time thinking about our new roles and what we could bring to each other. For Andy, who had been married before, it was an opportunity to sort things out anew. For Teri, who was marrying for the first time after many years of being single, the concept of joining presented many puzzles. As we sought guidelines, we searched our own experience, talked to many other married people, and scoured the bookstores. We found plenty of general marriage handbooks, but no guides specifically geared toward the issues of everyday life.

We've been authors, teachers, and personal growth trainers for many years. Of course, we've been students as well. As we have helped empower people to realize their potentials in several arenas, we realized a glaring deficiency. Nowhere was there a how-to for husbands. Many helpful theories and perspectives on the topic, but no specific reference works. Nothing to answer questions ranging from how to deal with recurring needs for intimacy (and autonomy) to "Should a husband open a car door for his wife?"

Well, like most people, we figured it out for ourselves. We have found that the attitudes and behaviors described in this book serve us well. Now we want to share them.

Teri & Andy Murphy, 1991-95
Arlington, Chico, Dunmore Town, St. George's

1

Three New Rules:
Make Your Marriage Strong
While Making Yourself Happy

Whether you are already married or are planning to be, think of your marriage as a play in the theater of your life. The part you have landed is The Husband. You are an actor in the finest sense; you *become* the role. You are also the creative genius of this play; you get to write your part. And best of all, you get the girl. *And on top of all this,* the role you create as Husband can make your marriage stronger while it makes you happier. What a deal!

Most of us, unfortunately, are either stuck with old scripts or have no clear sense of the roles we'd like to create. The traditional role sounded something like this:

- *A husband is the boss in the family.* (Although in one version, the wife only allows the husband to believe that he is the boss; she is the real power.)
- *A husband brings home the bacon.*
- *A husband keeps a stiff upper lip.*

The list goes on. When you landed the part of Husband, you may have decided that you didn't entirely like the old role, so you cast off some of its restrictions. Yet, you found it difficult to play the part without the old script. Actors need scripts. Without one, the old role has a way of slipping in, inviting one of you to be either manipulative or sacrificial.

New Rules Create New Roles

This book proposes that you establish a new role, a new playbook—one that's all your own. It encourages you to set it up so that the role you create, The

Husband, can make your marriage stronger while bringing you what you want and need most in life. Forget sacrifice and forget manipulation. We're talking you get to be happier while the marriage gets better.

The traditional roles were anchored in the belief that men and women are inherently different in predictable ways. Those who reject traditional roles argue that we learn our differences and we can unlearn them. Chances are, both positions are partly true. So we're going to propose something new to which you can anchor your role. It's a set of rules for looking at your marriage in a way that focuses on what you want and thus opens unlimited possibilities.

Rule 1: Assume You Are Together for a Purpose

This first rule—the Prime Directive—is the most important. It's an attitude that carries over into everything you do. It asks you to work from the premise that your marriage is no accident.

Some men believe their marriages were made in heaven. They *know* they were brought together for a reason. Perhaps you're one of these lucky ones. Or maybe you started out believing the heavens brought you the perfect wife, but that you or she has changed, and now you feel you're no longer with the "right" person. Maybe you even feel you got tricked into marrying the "wrong" person under pressure or for convenience.

Regardless of where you fit on this scale, you can get a lot of mileage by proceeding from the assumption that there is a purpose for your being with this woman.

Just think how this attitude changes things. If you believe your mating was an accident, a mistake, or just sexual attraction, fights about whether to leave the bedroom window open or closed at night remain just that—fights. But once you believe you're together for a reason, you have to start asking yourself, "Why are we fighting about this? What purpose does it serve?" Maybe it gives you a chance to be more cooperative, to learn patience, or even to be exposed to a different way of sleeping!

A Suggestion for Following Rule 1:

Use Everything for Your Learning
This precept was stated particularly well by Jon-Roger and Peter McWilliams in their excellent book, *Life 101*, in which they say: "Use everything for your upliftment, learning, and growth. Everything. Everything. Everything."

Want to have a good marriage—one that's secure, interesting, passionate, alive, and growing? You can't achieve these qualities by avoiding conflicts. The best route to a happy marriage is to tackle friction head on, indeed, to see every problem that arises as an opportunity for growth, personal and marital. (Remember that the Chinese symbol for *crisis* also translates as "a juncture providing opportunity.")

You particularly need to say what's hard to say. The more you tell yourself that you have to withhold something to avoid "rocking the boat," the more potential the truth probably has for growth and clearing the air. Honesty may feel risky, but it pays off, particularly when presented tactfully.

Suppose she has a habit that drives you nuts. She talks too loudly, recounts minute details when telling stories, repeatedly leaves drawers open or lights on after leaving a room. Anything—even more serious activities such as drinking or smoking too much. How can you use this for your learning? What might you learn from this experience? Some possibilities:

- *Assertiveness:* Confront the issue with her (tell her how you feel), without starting a fight.
- *Patience:* Feel solid and centered and not ruled by someone else's behavior.
- *Kindness:* See another's shortcomings and not judge them as "wrong."
- *Self-awareness:* Reflect on your own shortcomings; do you tell long-winded stories too?
- *Negotiating skills:* Reconcile your differences while keeping a cool head and your self-esteem.

There's something to learn in every experience. It'll make you a better man and a better husband. You are in charge of you. Anything and everything in your marriage, as in your life, can ultimately be used for your upliftment and growth. It's a winner's game.

● ● ●

Does Rule 1 mean no man is ever stuck with a mate who is "bad" for him, and no one should ever divorce under any circumstances? Of course not. Some marriages have such deeply embedded destructive patterns that one person acting alone may not be able to break free of them. And sometimes two people really do grow in such different directions that the purpose that brought them together can no longer be served. But before you quit, make sure you've given it everything you've got to find the good, the learning, the love you can bring to your marriage. Make sure you've studied this book carefully.

Remember that you guys chose each other for more reasons than physical attraction. Your marriage is the best of all routes for personal and spiritual growth.

Rule 2: Honor Your Differences

People are different. Your wife is the sum total of all her experiences, a unique expression of life. So are you. Honor her individuality by recognizing its uniqueness. Do the same for yourself.

When she sees events and relationships differently from your way, it's not because she's being disagreeable. It's who she is. Say she has a *problem* (your description) with cleanliness or promptness. She's either "Ms Super Clean," or she's "a slob." She's either "fidgeting and nervously early," or she's "always late."

Whenever she exhibits the "problem," notice how quickly your mind jumps to the idea, "She's wrong," or "She did that on purpose." She's not behaving this way to annoy you, any more than you behave the way you do to annoy her.

Of course, sometimes people do irritate each other on purpose. They play out aggressions and even get mean with each other, usually when some other area of life gets overwhelming or disappointing. But this is not what you are honoring. Honoring your differences doesn't mean you have to honor her bad moods, but rather the underlying person she is, through her ups and downs.

Mostly, she's just different. And the ways she differs from you are perfect for you. In his best selling couples book, *Getting the Love You Want,* Harville Hendrix advances the theory that in most marriages there is one critical difference between the partners, and it recurs in different forms. It may well be the thing both partners will admit they were attracted to originally. A quiet, easy going man, for example, may be attracted to an outgoing, vivacious woman because of her sparkling personality, only to be turned off later because she "talks too much," seeing her now as pushy and superficial. A meek woman may be attracted to a strong-willed man because he is such a "take charge" guy, only later she feels overwhelmed and ignored by his bossiness.

The central dissimilarity between you is likely to form a basis for all your major conflicts. After many years of research and work with couples, Hendrix says this difference is also the one that offers the greatest opportunity for growth and learning. The shy guy gets to learn about sparkle. Ms. meek is driven to learn to stand up for herself. Both have chosen the perfect mate to drive them crazy, OR to push the edge of the envelope of who they are.

Some Suggestions on How to Follow Rule 2:

Avoid Labels

The world's religions all agree on one issue: No judging. And that's what labeling is—judging. Beyond the theological reasons for suspending judgment (it's God's job) there's a practical reason as well: It doesn't work.

If you label your wife as "shallow" or "short-sighted" or "inconsiderate" you set yourself as the rule maker. Your notions are the standard by which all others are judged.

What happened the last time she judged you? Did you appreciate it? Did you thank her for pointing out how imperfect you were (according to her standards)? Did it improve your relationship? The best way to keep from being judged is not to judge. Labeling only makes it harder to work through differences.

Of all the best intentions, this seems to be the most difficult; many of us have to learn it and re-learn it all our lives. Still, it's worth the effort because labels cause resentment. And resentment is poison to your marriage. It has been said that when you hold it in your mind, you get paranoid. When you hold it in your body, you get sick. And when you hold it in your heart, you get mean.

Let Go of Expectations

Expectations are hopes that your wife is going to do a certain thing or become a certain way. They almost always cause problems.

When you got married, chances are you had a list in your head of some of her traits you weren't crazy about. Needs of yours she didn't fill. On some level, you probably told yourself she'd change. You also had a vision of how your life would be together.

For many men, the ideal wife is active, interesting, and attractive, and has just the right touch of independence. She's sensual to her husband's touch and attentive to his moods and needs in a lighthearted, often whimsical way. She looks great in her clothes. She can handle anything.

We're attracted to these ideals but in real life there's always something missing. We feel cheated and sometimes resentful when she doesn't measure up. Sometimes we compare her to other men's wives or even to our mother. We focus on what's missing, instead of what's there.

What's there is your wife. Embrace the uniqueness you and she bring to your marriage. Of course you learn from others, particularly those whose marriages you admire. But you don't have to live up to anyone else's model. This is your life. Figure out how you and your wife are going to experience it according to this guideline:

Agendas are okay. Expectations are not.

You may have on your agenda that your wife will develop an interest in sports and join you in the local softball league or in watching the NFL on Sundays. You'd love it if that happened, and you encourage it, letting her know what your agenda is. You do not, however, have the expectation that it will happen. Whatever happens is okay. You'll accept her choices for herself. *That's what Rule 2 is about.* Letting go of expectations frees you to enjoy your marriage for what is best about it without always comparing it to something else.

Rule 3: In All Things, Move Toward Her

Your marriage vows may have noted some opposite conditions (you know, sickness and health, richer and poorer, etc.). Fact is, most marriages have a little of both. Over your life together, there may even be extremes; she may get demanding or depressed, evangelical about some cause, perhaps even unbalanced. This rule advocates using every opportunity—the gloriously good as well as the not so good—to move toward her.

Often when things aren't going well, we pull away, feel resentful, or hide out. We may look as though we're engaging in family life, but we're actually holding back the best part of ourselves. There will certainly be times when you need space to cool off or collect your thoughts. You may just need *alone* time; most people do. Go ahead and take it. But make it short. The longer you're "apart," the more work it will take to convince her to rejoin you. Usually when you feel the urge to bolt, it's a good sign that you need to drop your armor and link arms with her as soon as possible.

You may be tempted to say, "What about *her* part in this? Isn't she supposed to hold up her end? I can't do it all." True, but this is not a wife's manual.

Besides, you can't control what she does—only what you do. In addition, you may find that once you shift your stance, even slightly, it produces a surprising shift in her.

A suggestion for following Rule 3:

Take Responsibility for Your Own Happiness
Your wife can't *make* you happy and you can't *make* her happy. Each of us is personally responsible for that elusive state.

Ever met a man who saw the best in life? He turns lemons into lemonade, finds silver linings in dark clouds, sees the finest qualities in people (instead of focusing on their faults). He may even have a wife whom other people consider unattractive or obnoxious. But he focuses on her good side and finds ways to cope with the rest. He's responsible for his own happiness. So are you.

Then there's your wife's happiness. You, naturally, are interested in having your wife be content, fulfilled, and gratified by life. You want to keep unpleasantness out of her life. A noble quest—one which will keep you busy and be its own reward. It's also impossible.

You can provide all the necessary ingredients for her happiness, but she has to experience it herself. She's responsible for her experience of life. Should you stop trying, become inattentive, or neglect her? Absolutely not. That's not moving toward her in all things. The point of this suggestion is to keep you sane whenever she isn't happy.

She's got her own set of hang-ups, of problems at work and with the kids (and sometimes with you), of unresolved conflicts with parents, siblings, and friends. Childhood events influence her reactions and responses to life, just as yours do to you.

You are not responsible *for* her, you are responsible *to* her.

You are responsible for yourself and for your part in the integrity of your marriage. Move toward her: support, encourage, assist, love, and honor your wife, but remember, you can't *make* her happy. She has to do that for herself.

You have to do it for yourself, too.

So How Should a Man Behave?

What do these rules mean for the traditional role of Husband? This is where you get to write the script; the answer is, it's up to you. Right now is a good time to see how you define yourself as a man. Use the three rules to assess your beliefs and decide which parts you want to keep and which you want to redefine.

Your attitudes toward traditional roles needn't cause you to reject or embrace them entirely. If you're going to throw some out, make sure you replace them with others that truly serve you both. Pick which ones serve you best.

Even if you and your wife take wholly traditional roles in your family, you can be "liberated" from the bonds of history and social convention *if* you both actively participate in the process of choosing. In other words, as co-directors of this play, decide together how you'll interpret your roles. Many old traditions work well for people, and by consciously choosing them, we make them our own. You guys are writing the script.

Shape your role to serve the goals of your marriage. Of course that means you'll have to get clear on what these goals are.

Your Goals

You wouldn't try to run a business without a business plan. So why try to run a marriage without something similar? What are the dreams and values you share? If you've always taken it for granted that you both know what they are, you may be surprised at how much benefit there can be in spelling them out. What do you stand for as a unit, a team?

Talk this over with your wife and ask her to join you in establishing your goals in a Joint Vision Statement like the one at the back of this book. Whether you come up with many goals or only a few, this endeavor can provide you with a new level of strength and pride in your marriage. One thing is for certain: If you work together on common goals with a common vision, you will have a life far richer than either of you can achieve alone. It's the best kind of synergy. And whatever your goals are, the new rules can help you achieve them. Living by them will serve you and strengthen your marriage.

• • •

Rule 1: Assume You Are Together for a Purpose

Rule 2: Honor Your Differences

Rule 3: In All Things, Move Toward Her

Now that you know the new rules, the challenge is to put them into practice. The remainder of this book offers suggestions for applying the rules to common situations in married life. Of course, your life and your wife are unique. No book could cover every situation you'll face. If you find you have a problem that isn't covered by a chapter, go back to the three rules. They may seem difficult at first, but there's nothing you can't handle. Take your time and keep rehearsing. You'll find you get better and better at your co-starring role and at applying the rules. You've got your whole life to polish your performance.

2

Asking For Change

How much longer, Jill? If we don't leave in the next 5 minutes, we're going to be late. Why can't you ever get ready on time?

Had much success using an observation like that? Probably not. People don't like to be pressured or criticized; in fact, they often dig in their heels and behave the opposite of the requested change. Poorly worded requests for change usually fail. The good news is, there's a way to do it right.

You've known since you were 12 that you can't *make* someone change. Oh, you forget once in a while and try to change people (like your wife) by silent treatments or threats or guilt trips, but you know in your heart that people only change by their own will, and because they see the value on their own, not because they've been ordered to.

So, if you can't *make* your wife change, what can you do? You can present a good case, let her decide on her own, and not get in the way. Here are the steps to follow in asking for change:

1. **Lay some groundwork**. If there's any chance she'll resist this change, no matter how small a request, smooth the road—grease the skids. You're not about to condemn her; you're simply requesting some new behavior. Starting with a little praise goes a long way. Then explain your reasons for the request, and don't get in your own way doing it.
   There's something I'd to talk to you about. Is this an okay time? I really appreciate how you keep the kids from waking me on Saturdays when I like to sleep late. I know it's not an easy job. What I'd also like to ask is..... (state your request clearly)

2. **State your request in simple, straightforward words**. Here's what I would like you to do, and here's why. Since this is often difficult, it's a good idea to rehearse, or at least decide exactly what it is you want. Make it reasonable, do-able, and timely; e.g., don't say, "I want you to lose 30 pounds by next week." Similarly, don't talk about lateness on your way out the door. And say please.

3. **Tell her what's in it for you**.
   - *I would really enjoy having extra time together with you; that's why I'm asking you to change your schedule.*
   - *I'd feel more comfortable if you didn't tell those private details of our life when we're out in public. I could get to know your friends better if I felt more at ease.*
   - *I feel ignored when you look away while we're discussing something. I can concentrate better when you look as though you're paying attention.*

Pretending that your request is only for *her* good is dishonest; you have a personal reason for wanting her to do something differently. If you think you don't have one, think again. Be honest; you've got nothing to be ashamed of.

Sometimes, a wish for someone else to change is a good opportunity to examine something in ourselves.

   Why is this important to me?
   What does this tell me about me?
   Maybe I need to meet her half-way, or more.

4. **Tell her what you think is in it for her**, but make sure you've followed Step 3 first. Be aware that she may not see things the same way you do. Remember that people do things for emotional as well as logical reasons.

5. **Explain the consequences as you foresee them**.
   a. If she changes, how will things be different? How will it affect you and your marriage? *If you do this, I'll be happier and I think we'll get along better.*
   b. If she doesn't change, how will things be? Realism is better than melodrama here.
      If you don't, I'll continue to be uneasy.
      I won't like it, but I can try to live with it.
   c. Tell her honestly what you absolutely can't live with, too. There may be some behaviors she must change, like abusive behavior towards children, alcoholism, etc.
   d. Be prepared to negotiate. (See the chapter on Negotiating.)

Your language can be your best ally if you can teach yourself to use "I" statements—phrases that focus on how you feel instead of what she's done wrong. She can't take offense if all you do is report on how her behavior affects you, and then request a do-able change.

It seems to me you often change your mind about what to wear just before we go out, which tends to make us late. When this happens, I feel irritated and I get restless; I start out for a party in a bad mood. I'd like you to plan ahead more, to allow enough time to get ready. Is there something I can do to help?

This kind of SNAG[1] language may sound awkward, but it's better for your marriage than being a bully or sullenly shutting her out.

How your attitude comes through will be much more important than getting the steps exactly right. Mostly it's important to avoid any sense that you are judging her. There's plenty of precedent for condemning the sin and not the sinner. When a child is naughty, it's the wayward behavior we denounce, not the child. Treat your wife with even more respect and dignity. Speak only to behaviors and attitudes in these requests, not to what you think is wrong in her personality. She's an independent, thinking being who is deciding her own directions in life—just as you are. If you want her to change, respect this.

A husband asks for changes the way he'd like to be asked.

---

[1] Sensitive New Age Guy

3

Being Alone

Tom and Tina have exacting careers; each loves the other and their daughter Rachel; each strives to keep their love and their marriage alive. Vacations, having friends over, visits to grandparents, and late-night dinner with wine in front of the fire are all wonderful, shared activities. But they need something else. Neither gets enough time alone. Each needs time totally separate from the role of carpenter/ husband/father and journalist/wife/mother. Not just a nap or a late sleep-in on Saturday morning, but a solitary walk. Not just quiet time in front of the TV, but meditative time with no distractions. Tom sometimes feels he has to "sneak" this time into his schedule—walking home the long way, getting up early for a quiet time with the newspaper, on occasion stopping for a beer after work but blaming the delay on heavy traffic. He feels uneasy about the fact that he likes being alone sometimes.

Everybody needs some time alone on a regular basis. In addition to that kind of alone time, there will no doubt be times in your married life when you and your wife are apart. Jobs, other family commitments, illness, or perhaps the need for a personal retreat will mean occasionally sleeping under separate roofs. Sometimes it's inevitable; sometimes it's even advisable. Either way, your job is to make it work.

Alone time is one of the areas most likely to emphasize the differences in you and your wife's needs for intimacy and autonomy. (See the chapter Having it Both Ways.) So, it's almost inevitable that one of you will feel the discomfort of separation more acutely than the other.

Start by understanding that being alone may mean something different to each of you:

Being alone is difficult.

- If this is true for you, admit it. If you or she is out of town, you may be "too busy to notice," but you know whom you're not snuggled-up next to. Tell her how you feel. *I don't like being away from you; I'd rather be able to kiss you goodnight.* Be aware of the effect your need has on her.
- If it's true for her, be compassionate. Know that she may need special comfort and reassurance of your love. As you've probably already figured out, resisting her needs in this area only intensifies them. Instead of dismissing her with *You know I had to make this trip,* you could say, *I'm having a good time here, but I'm really looking forward to having you back in my arms.*

Being alone is rejuvenating.

- If this is true for you, take comfort in it. You need this alone time to re-energize, to collect your thoughts, to get yourself back together. Whether it's a business trip or a hike in the woods, use this time to its best advantage, and tell her of its value. She needs to understand what this means to you. If you are calling from a distant place on a business trip, it's much better that she hear the words, *I loved exploring the city alone today,* and not that she hear a tone of voice she might interpret as *Boy am I glad to be away from you for a few days.*
- If it's true for her that being alone is rejuvenating, understand it and make sure she has the opportunity to enjoy it. Don't let it threaten you or your trust. If you've got some reason to mistrust her, address that issue and deal with it directly, but don't misinterpret the human need for time alone.

You are a couple, but you are two individuals as well, each personally responsible for yourself. Having and taking advantage of alone time is an important way to deal with that responsibility. Find time every day (or every week) when you are physically and mentally alone with yourself. You both have the right to this time. Your job is to find that space for yourself and to encourage and accommodate her needs, too. If she's working and carrying most of the responsibility for the household, it's your job to help her find the time she needs.

Talk to her about this right to alone, and take care that you don't fall into habits that make it impossible to accomplish. Keep your priorities straight for the sake of your marriage, your personal growth, and your sanity.

A husband makes time for himself.

4

Being an In-law

What would your family say if they knew you were reading a book about how to be a husband?

• • •

Where did your mind automatically go in response to the term *family* in that question? Was it to your Mom and Dad and the rest of the extended family you were born into? Or was it to your wife and perhaps children? Were your brothers and sisters in the picture?

You bring a family with you into your marriage. Even when some (or a lot) of its members are dead or completely out of touch, they still comprise your mind's image of *family*. This image creates expectations of how family life should be.

Family means all the important folks on your side plus all the important folks on her side. You are part of a larger family now. If you're lucky, it has enriched your life and you have enriched it. If you're like most folks, the new family also brought a few problems. Either way, being an in-law has no doubt complicated your life. To make the most of your in-law role, here are some tips:

1. **Honor the old; welcome the new.** Along with the ready-made families we bring with us into our marriages, we also bring expectations. We expect to celebrate certain rites and holidays in certain ways. Even those married for a while automatically eat meals according to a certain ritual because, "That's the way we always did it in my family."

The types of gifts you give, what you eat on Sunday evening, the way you have of expressing (or not expressing) true feelings—all these practices were common to your family. And neither you nor the family you came from expects

15

you to behave any differently just because you're married. Even after years!

These traditions have some significance in your life, and it's important that you honor them. But beware of getting locked into believing that your original family's way is the right way. It's just as important that you honor some of your wife's traditions, and that you be open to creating new ones. One of the most rewarding things about building a new family is that it offers an opportunity to bring new traditions into being.

2. **Keep your priorities straight**. As you sort out all the minute details of life, remember that the top priority in the world of in-laws is your wife. *Your mother starts criticizing your wife about a number of small things and has begun taking advantage of her good nature. It's a delicate line to walk. You don't want to alienate Mom, but your wife has asked you to intercede.*

Look to your wife's needs first. She is number one because your family at its most basic unit is you and she. Use your best sonly diplomacy in dealing with your mother and in helping them get along, but remember who has top priority: the woman you married.

Suppose conflicts arise from her side of the family—they disapprove of you, are always meddling, or act in ways that ruin family gatherings. Recognize that such clashes, at their root, are probably not truly aimed at you. They may have had other expectations for her, and if you didn't fill all of them, they'll find some way to express disappointment. And it may take years for them to know you as well as they know her. Everyone knows that families are complicated (and most have a few jerks, too). Take a look at your side of the family. Anything unusual about how some of them get along? The same is true for her side. Your job is to understand this fact of life and to keep your priorities straight. As you struggle with whose needs to put first, remember that the basic core of this family unit is you and she.

Naturally, you'll expect her to be in your corner when conflicts arise—just as you will always be in hers. But take care. If you consistently end up in fights with your in-laws and then make her side with you out of loyalty, step back and wonder. What else is going on here? *Am I testing her love? How does this serve our marriage?*

3. **Learn from the family.** When you and your in-laws are in conflict—for whatever reason—go the extra mile. This doesn't mean becoming a door-mat; you still have your own personal and immediate family consider-ations. But the fact is that these people are now a part of your family. If you extend to them the Prime Directive of Rule 1 (that they are in your life for a purpose, just as your wife is), you'll have new opportunities for learning and growth. That attitude is more likely to smooth things for you than believing you got stuck with your in-laws through bad luck.

So, don't forget to learn. If your mother-in-law is a difficult person to get along with, it may be an opportunity to learn unconditional love. If your brother-in-law seems to need to outdo you in categories such as Money Earned or Things Acquired, it may be an opportunity to define and defend what success means to you. Cantankerous people outside of a family can be ignored; cross fathers-in-law cannot be so easily overlooked. Ask yourself, *What can I learn from this?* Directness with diplomacy? Honesty with kindness? Openness with tact?

Assume it's not a mistake that you're their in-law.

4. **Be a family builder.** Your marriage created a new family. You chose her, and with her came her family. Now they're part of your family. Take that word to heart: *family.* Think of members of her family as part of yours, because they are. It's not *them* and *us.* You're all a part of a larger family. And since you and your wife are responsible for bringing all these people under the same family umbrella, it's your job to build toward this goal.

As a newcomer to her side of the family, perhaps you can bring a fresh perspective and neutral stance to long-simmering conflicts. Don't underestimate your power to do this no matter how they have (or haven't) accepted you.

A husband aims for the ideal where the two existing families blend in a spirit of acceptance and love. You've got a lifetime to work toward this.

A husband is a family man.

5

Being the Man of the House

Who wears the pants in your family? That old quip questions which spouse has authority, and you know that there is no single authority on this team. Neither of you is boss. But you are the man of the house—a role that carries certain demands and requires certain qualities. Being the man of the house has three aspects: it's about action, strength, and responsibility.

A man's relationship with his wife is first of all, an active one. In order to procreate, he must act by inseminating her egg. This actor role is not only true biologically, it also serves as a metaphor for the husband-wife relationship.

This doesn't make you the boss. It also doesn't imply that her part is in any way lesser than yours. You'll both decide on your life together. After all, you're partners in this venture. Co-equal partners.

It does mean, however, that in order to cause things to happen, someone needs to act. Once you decide where to go, someone needs to put the key into the ignition, turn it on, and drive. Action makes it happen.

Will she drive, too? Or make the airline reservations or get the car serviced or perform any of the hundreds of other supposedly man-of-the-house jobs? Of course she will. You'll naturally work out some system whereby she activates certain parts of your life while you initiate others. It makes good sense to do it that way.

You're both responsible for the action, the motion in your marriage, but you can only control you. Whenever she chooses not to act, for whatever reason, pick up the ball. Act. Do it because it's the right thing, and it will serve you both.

A husband is a man of action.

19

• • •

Strength, too, underlies the role of the man of the house. On balance, most husbands are physically stronger than their wives, and there's nothing wrong with that. There's nothing wrong with the opposite, either. Who can open a jar or carry the heaviest luggage is not what true strength is about.

It's about keeping physically and mentally fit. It's about maintaining your strength of will and strength of character. It's about being able to participate fully in your life with her, make love with her, do your equitable share of the labor, maintain your health. (And not just for your own well being; she needs you to be your best.)

When problems arise, go at them. You came into this world whole, complete, and perfect. Draw on the strength of that truth. "Be all that you can be" is more than just an Army recruitment slogan. It's sound, husbandly advice.

A husband is strong man of action.

• • •

Anyone who dismisses the men's movement in this country is missing a good bet. Poets such as Robert Bly and other leaders of this movement are urging men to take a fresh look at some of the most ancient and mythical traditions and symbols of manhood. This doesn't mean returning to old ways but rather reclaiming the personal strengths some men lost touch with in the process of opening new roles for the women in their lives. This reclamation may require some redefining.

When warriors of yesterday would sound the battle cry,
Readying their weapons for the fight,
For victory and glory, they'd be prepared to die;
A test of skill, bravery, and might.

But the deeper battle is not of swords and guns,
Or even who is right and who is wrong.
The battle is within us, in becoming who we are;
Hearing inner guidance clear and strong.

Warriors of the heart,
Standing in the truth of who we are,
Called forth by vision, sworn to play our part,
We are warriors, warriors of the heart.

These wonderful lyrics by Stephen Longfellow Fiske and Jai Joseph recommend a forthright, undaunted pose. The man of the house stands tall and courageous in facing the fears and doubts that come during every marriage. He's up to the responsibility.

The warrior within you supplies you with the inner strength to "stand in the truth of who you are"; to take responsibility for your life, your choices, your experiences—not with praise or blame (there's no judgment here) but with the accountability that comes with knowing you are in control of yourself. Be the best husband you can and don't blame events or other people for who you are. You're the only one in charge of the man of the house.

The man of the house—The Husband—is a strong and responsible man of action.

6

Bill Paying, Bookkeeping, & Record Keeping

Scott sits at the desk in the corner of the den and pulls the bank statement from the middle left drawer. He'd stored it there just yesterday after sorting the mail. The calculator in easy reach, a sharpened pencil, a post-dinner mug of decaf, Scott was ready: Balancing the checkbook had begun.

It's a bit tricky. Diane writes checks from a book she carries in her purse. She's pretty good about recording amounts and payees, but sometimes she forgets. Not on purpose, of course.

So he carefully compares the bank statement with the canceled checks and marks the checkbook when they match. The complexity of Scott and Diane's life shows up in this monthly event, and 45 minutes pass before Scott returns to the planet.

During that ³/₄ hour Scott was transported into the world of math as though the Enterprise had beamed him aboard. In that world, he was totally, happily absorbed.

In the ideal situation, one or the other of you is Scott (the accountant/bookkeeper type), and that person enjoys paying the bills, balancing the checkbook—anything having to do with the family records. He or she is probably already doing it. It's the ideal. There should be no problems. But, of course, there are.

Scott bristles when Diane "doesn't appreciate how hard it is to keep the finances straight," when she bounces a check or loses receipts or misfiles—or any number of things which he considers important. He even feels put upon or unappreciated and occasionally suggests that Diane should take her turn at the task.

Cut it out, guys.

Scott, you need to learn patience. She's not out to sabotage you or your efforts. She doesn't even hate the numbers. She just doesn't care about them the same way you do. Take extra pains to ensure that you get the figures and papers you need, and do this without patronizing her.

If your wife is playing Scott's role in this activity, then help her get what she needs. Your family needs these books kept, these bills paid, etc., and she is the one charged with it. Help her. It's difficult to do this job with less than full cooperation from the other partner: Record every check you write. Write legibly. Save all receipts in a special box.

But suppose your situation is less than ideal? Suppose both of you want to be Scott; in other words, be in charge of the money?

The quickest-to-mind solution is to have one person do the whole job for a month, a quarter, or a year, and then switch. Take turns. Of course, you'll have to guard against comparing who did it better.

What might be of more value is to find a way to work together. Chances are, your level of tension about this indicates there's something in it both of you could learn from. It may represent a power struggle for control of money. If so, this is a great opportunity to confront fears of losing control. The situation has presented itself for a reason.

Once you put it in that light, you'll be able to think of several ways you can work together. Divide the whole job into modules and each take half, for example. Or one pays the fixed monthly bills, and the other pays the credit card bills. Or consider two accounts; then trade modules after a while. Work with each other actively. Too complicated, too inefficient for your busy lives, you say? Make the time. What you'll gain has far greater impact on your union than just the balancing of books

.Finally, suppose that neither of you wants to be Scott. You both feel unmoved by numbers, and you both wish it would all go away. Of course, it still needs to get done. Some possible solutions: Hire someone. (It's only a few hours a month, especially for a professional.) Trade favors with a friend or family member; you mow her lawn and she does your books. Sit down together once a week and make it a joint project; reward yourselves when you've finished. You'll come up with an appropriate prize. Get creative.

If all else fails, you do it. Take a class at a local adult education center to learn how. Even if you already have the skills, take a class anyway; it'll put you around people in similar circumstances which will help energize you.

You know you don't like doing it, but DO IT ANYWAY. The situation presents you both with the opportunity to take some responsibility. Move this stalemate off center, accept the responsibility, and act decisively.

Learn to like it, too. Performing this monthly (or weekly) activity grudgingly, resignedly, or grumpily will not serve your marriage. Tell yourself: It's not a sacrifice; I'm being a responsible husband. And being a husband is a great job. Not always easy, but great.

A husband keeps his life in order.

7

Breadwinning aka Providing

How should the bread be won? Where does the money come from to afford your life style? Well, here's where you get to confront some fears and figure out one of your more important roles as husband. Your responsibility to your family—the most basic social commitment in your life—helps define you both to yourself and to the rest of the world. Your job is to take care of your family. The fun part is defining "take care of."

Start by asking an impertinent question of yourself: Who "should" provide the income?

Do I believe that the husband must be the principal breadwinner? That wives should participate fully in the breadwinning? That the husband and wife should each contribute according to his or her ability?

In this increasingly complex world, we rarely hear the phrase "He's a good provider" said of a husband, anymore. If, however, a couple decides that the husband should be the main or sole provider, why not?

The classic nuclear family (Dad has the job, Mom stays home with the kids) is still alive and thriving. In many families, this is the life style of choice. And there's nothing wrong with it! It's a valid choice—one that makes sense to a lot of people, especially those raising families.

But what if you don't or can't earn as much as she does? Perception may be your biggest problem. Does your immediate world (friends or family or that little voice inside) perceive you as unmanly if you are not the main provider? Doesn't logic dictate that each person contribute equitably? Doesn't your heart also tell you this?

25

The truth is it doesn't matter who earns more money. What matters is that you—the husband—are making a full contribution to providing for your family. This may include spending quality time with them, providing them with a stable and ordered environment, or taking time out to develop talents that will enrich all your lives or assure your future. And some of these ways of providing for them could be in conflict with making more money.

There's no praise or blame for the money-making part; it needs to get done, so you do it the best way you can. Whether you or she earns more money, or if some other outside source of yours or hers covers your living expenses, SO WHAT? Both of you are responsible for providing for this family. Being the principal breadwinner is not a manly (or womanly) trait. It's just life and how you decide to assign duties. Work it out between you.

If you're having a great deal of difficulty doing so, it may be time to ask a bigger, more impertinent question.

What does money mean to me? Underneath the obvious answers (It pays the rent and feeds us), is it also a symbol for power? And if so, how much power do I need in my marriage?

The link between money and power jumps right out at you. Evidence abounds in our world that the one with the most money wields the most power. Thus, the one who "provides" the most is seen as the potent one.

You two are not together so that one can dominate the other. You're together because you are the best person for her, and she's the best person for you. Power struggles distract from the more important growth you two are capable of. Let your power flow from the strength of being united. From that position of strength, you will be better able to provide for *all* your family's needs. You may also be surprised to find that when you shift the equation from "How can I earn more?" to "How can I best contribute as a member of this team?" you open up different possibilities for achieving all your goals. Including the one of simply getting the family fed.

Since the root of so many marital problems is money, it's worth your time and energy to work on this issue. Don't let old, misguided assumptions about husbands, wives, and money get in the way of your happy union.

The lessons we all have to learn from dealing with money at home are so important that they'll probably cause you frustration from time to time. The most vital stuff is usually the hardest to learn. Stay at it. If you're still having trouble, read the chapter on Resisting.

A husband provides for his family.

8

Changing

Change!? You've got to be kidding.
What you see is what you get.
I'm too set in my ways to change, now.
Love me as I am.

Some people want to stay the same all their lives, as though there were some prize for hanging onto the identity forged as a teenager. There isn't. Besides, how is anyone going to improve himself without at least a little remodeling now and then?

The best kind of marriage is one in which you influence each other for the better. Trouble is, this means you both have to be open to changing. While lots of folks enjoy a change of scene or a change of pace, almost no one welcomes a change in himself or herself. Deserved or not, husbands have a bad reputation in this regard. For you to welcome the changes that your wife can bring about in you may take an almost heroic and continuing act of will.

Of course, this doesn't mean you should welcome all changes. Try consulting the following process when you consider a change that she has requested.

Translate

When your wife wants you to change something, she won't always be articulate. If she exasperatedly says, "Why can't you be neater?" you know she's not truly asking you to explain something; she's asking you to try being a little tidier. Don't jump on her for the way she asked it.

Think about the last time you made a snide or critical remark toward her.

She has some behaviors you wish she didn't have. You wish she'd change some things, and you've even told her some of them. (Lovingly, of course, if you read the chapter on Asking for Change.) Some, however, you haven't told her. You've kept them to yourself because they were too little or unimportant or you just couldn't be bothered or you didn't want to risk an argument. Sometimes they snuck out "on their own," and you said something hurtful without having planned to.

The point is, If *you* are not always articulate about your wishes and feelings, how do you expect *her* to be? Be aware that people aren't always able to express their desires eloquently. In other words, sometimes she'll get snippy.

Your first job may be to translate.

If she says petulantly, "Why do you always have to be so cold to my mother?" resist your combative instinct. You may want to challenge her use of "always" or come back contentiously with some snappy rejoinder. You may want to accuse her of some slight of which she is guilty. You may even righteously ignore her. You are reacting to an accusation.

Instead, read what's behind her outburst. You wish she'd do it more directly and with tact, but she hasn't. You can interpret and respond accordingly even though she hasn't said it the way you want. You can still understand her. She's requesting a change.

Move through any barriers to the communication. Above all, don't compound a difficult situation by distancing yourself. Respond to the real issue, the underlying request in her statement. Project your love and understanding. Maybe she's just being cranky.

Reach for the higher ground. You know what she's trying to say. Help her turn a criticism into a request for change. "So, I guess you think I should be more understanding and nicer to your Mom." Maybe she'll do the same for you when you next go inarticulate and mouth-off about something. Figure out what's going on and project your understanding. You love her, remember?

Assess What's at Stake

Ask her to make a case for why you should change. Knowing her motives may help you get clear on what you want to do. Some changes, whether easily made or not, will improve your life together; others won't. Ask yourself a couple of questions to help sort out what's at stake:

Question 1: How might this change serve me (or us)?

No matter what her motives are, you may find some benefit in changing. Have you thought about making this change before? Have other people mentioned it, too? Do you seem to resist this change frequently? Hard as it is to admit, this change may be in your best interests. Or it may not.

The very fact that your wife asked you is important. If she wants you to have particular skills (tolerance with the children), to develop a certain mastery (barbecuing, shelf-building, etc.), or to stop an annoying habit (cracking your knuckles), consider it. She's your wife.

Avoid the opposite temptation: Resisting the change (even if it's good for you) *because* your wife asked you. In other words, don't allow foolish pride to interfere with your judgment.

Look always to enrich your marriage. If this change will both enrich your life and please your wife, then it definitely will serve your marriage. The two seem intertwined. What serves both of you, serves you individually, and vice versa.

Question 2: Am I willing to make the change?

Some changes don't cost you much, particularly if they don't affect your sense of yourself; in other words, they're no big deal. If she wants you to call to let her know you're going to be home late, you can probably do so without losing self-esteem or giving up part of who you are. Whereas if she wants you to be more expressive of your feelings, and you pride yourself on being non-emotional, the cost to you may be higher. Much higher. Are you willing to pay it? Can you expand your sense of who you are in order to accommodate a new behavior? Weigh the benefits and the costs and know that you're the one deciding. Make sure you act out of choice not habit.

Decide

Your intuition is as important as your logic when it comes to deciding. Trust both parts of yourself. If a change seems to serve both you and your relationship, and if the cost to you is worth it, you'll probably want to change. If the benefit is unclear or the cost feels too high, you may decide to say no. You have the right.

Your next job is to respond to the request. At the minimum, be clear. When you choose a course of action (to change, not to change, to compromise, etc.), explain your intent straightforwardly, and remember to move toward her in all things (Rule 3). She may or may not love your choice, but she has a right to understand what you're going to do and why.

I know you wish I'd spend time with you as soon as we get home from work, but that's the hour when I most enjoy peace and quiet. That time is important to me.

But *if and when* you start working on a change, do it wholeheartedly. Remind yourself why you're doing it. Don't keep score, either. A change on your part does not mean that she is now required to do likewise.

Be intrepid. A husband does not fear change.

9

Complimenting

In one of the steamier scenes from "Star Trek; the Next Generation," young Ensign Crusher, a teenager, asks the more experienced First Officer Riker to teach him how to talk to girls. Riker invites the exotic Guinan, a wise older woman, to help him demonstrate his technique:

Riker: *You are the most beautiful woman in the galaxy—Your eyes are like stars*

Crusher: *(rolling his eyes in disbelief) Sorry guys, this is not my style...*

Guinan: *(forgetting this is just a role play) Shut up kid. Now, what were you saying about my eyes?*

Never underestimate the power of a compliment. Your compliments may not be designed to turn your wife into putty, but when they're used frequently and well, compliments make the giver and receiver feel good. They can be a source of joy and support in your marriage.

So, start with the premise that giving and receiving compliments are both desirable. Since you can't control what you receive, concentrate on giving and on *how* you receive. Not all compliments are created equal.

WHAT TO COMPLIMENT

1. **Good: Something she has little or no control over;** e.g., height, gorgeous hair or skin, eye color, figure, etc. Telling your wife how much you love her great looking legs may delight her, but remember she hasn't personally accomplished anything here. She just had good leg genes.

31

2. **Better: Something she has added to her external self;** e.g., make up, jewelry, clothing, hair style, etc. Be attentive to what she wears and how she looks, and tell her what you like and appreciate. She has taken time and thought in these additions, and part of the reason is to please you. If you don't care for a certain outfit, express your thoughts kindly, and compliment something else.

3. **Best: Something she has accomplished;** e.g., her skills at listening, dancing, sharing, art, cooking, making love, singing, caring for you, mothering, gardening—the list is endless. Compliment these talents particularly at those moments when you are feeling uplifted by them.

With any luck, you learned the value of giving and receiving compliments at an early age. If you didn't, it's not too late to learn how to do both.

If you're ever uneasy receiving compliments (especially ones from your wife), look at some of the reasons why:

- Feeling Indebted: I don't like the feeling that I have to return her compliment.
- The "imposter syndrome": I don't really deserve that compliment. She just thinks I'm a good public speaker because she's in love with me.
- Ulterior motives: Why is she saying such nice things about me? What's behind this ploy? I won't offer any compliments, lest she suspect my motives.
- Humility: My parents taught me not to toot my own horn. I don't encourage this in others; they may get conceited.
- Equality: People who are peers don't offer compliments because that momentarily puts the complimenter/praiser in a superior position. A man complimented for doing a certain job well may feel uneasy. I've done this well all my life; why is she complimenting me now? Does she think this gives her the right to criticize me tomorrow?

Well, it's time to get past all that. Compliments are offered as praise, admiration, or flattery; they are courteous and respectful. What could be better than soaking them up from your wife?

So, compliment your wife often. She'll like it, it'll make your life easier, and she'll probably respond by complimenting you more often. When she does, say words that add up to "Thank you." More and more, you'll find you enjoy it.

A husband gives and receives compliments generously and naturally.

10

Criticizing

Criticize:
  (a) to analyze and evaluate objectively
  (b) to find fault, reproach, and generally disapprove

Notice the difference between these two dictionary definitions. The fact is, you're going to criticize your wife, and she's going to criticize you. The trick is to use definition (a), not (b). Try thinking of it as something else, *feedback*, for example. But, whatever you call it, don't pretend it's not criticism. When you comment on *what* she says and *how* she says it, when you wonder out loud if she shouldn't have done something differently, when you question her reasons for acting or not acting, you're criticizing. It's okay—As long as you follow some guidelines.

But first, distinguish this activity from *asking for change*. If you want to talk about her behavior toward other people—third parties—you're criticizing, or at least critiqueing. If it's about her behavior toward you, you may want to go to the chapter "Asking for Change."

Guidelines for Criticizing (Giving Feedback to) Your Wife:

  1. **Come from love**. Take a 2-second visit to your motives before you offer the observations. Do you want to prove her illogical? Silly? Wrong? If so, you need to flip your energy. Get on her side of the table for a moment. What can you say—fruitfully—that will serve her?
  When you said that to Dick tonight, it sounded as though you wanted him to feel guilty. You must be pretty upset; that's not like you.

2. **Get rid of** *shoulds* **and** *shouldn'ts.* Telling her what she should do or feel (or shouldn't do or feel) is not a good idea. Instead, show by your tone of voice and choice of words that you are not judging or disapproving of her. If you *are* judging or disapproving, stop it. It never works; it only pisses her off. Ask her how she thinks/feels about things. Indicate your confidence that she can handle the situation herself.
   You seem to be avoiding your sister since that incident at the party. Are you still upset? You're usually so good about making up with her.

3. **Focus on behavior**. If you've got a complaint, voice it, but direct it toward behavior she can do something about. Suggest an alternative.
   It seemed to me that Ruby was offended when you made that comment about her new job. Perhaps if you tell her you used to work nights too, she'll realize you were actually being sympathetic.

4. **Time it right and make sure she wants it**. (See the chapter Solving Her Problems.) She may not be open to your judgments. (Are you usually open to hers?) If she's not, your criticism is doomed to failure. All she'll get is defensive; you'll feel misunderstood, and then you'll both stew. Don't keep doing what doesn't work. Remember that one of the definitions of INSANITY is "repeating a behavior over and over while expecting it to have a different result." Don't expect her to welcome your suggestions or comments unless you've satisfied the first three of these Guidelines.

When She Criticizes You

You don't like being criticized any more than she does. When your wife gives you feedback, if she fails to follow these guidelines, point them out. Discuss how they might benefit you both. You're here to help each other learn. In the best-case scenario, your perceptions and experience can provide new insights to her, as hers can to you. Perhaps you can patiently help each other learn some valuable lessons.

A husband criticizes the way he wants to be criticized.

11

Deciding Small Stuff

Which movie do you feel like seeing?
What should we serve our dinner guests?
How should we celebrate your birthday tomorrow?
When do you want to open our Christmas presents?

A small decision—like one of those above—is best left in the hands of the spouse to whom it makes the biggest difference.

In most matters affecting you both, one of you will "have more energy" or feel more impassioned about the decision than the other. If deep inside, you really don't care where the chair goes or what color to paint the living room (and if she does care), she gets the nod....even if it means you have to paint the room.

You've probably already noticed that the real problems come when one of you "makes a big deal" out of everything or when one of you never seems to care.

If you are the one to whom things always seem to be a big deal, ask yourself *Am I being honest? Does it really make a big difference to me whether we have Thanksgiving dinner in the afternoon or in the evening, or am I using my stance on this to prove or protect some other position?*

If your spouse senses the latter, you can bet she'll suddenly start caring more about when the turkey goes on the table.

Check your motives. See if what is truly small stuff repeatedly turns up feeling like big stuff. Here's a trick for catching whether you've got "too much" energy on something. In his thought-provoking book, *Getting the Love You Want,* Harville Hendrix suggests watching for the words "always" and "never."

You never want to take a walk with me.
We always have to open presents your way.

Statements like these are usually tipoffs to some bigger underlying complaint, perhaps a power struggle. Deal with that separately; don't let it influence every little thing you do. Deciding is not about winning and losing, it's about accommodating. Who cares the most?

The trick is to avoid keeping score. If she's had more "nods" than you lately, don't be combative about it. Keep competition out of it. Making small decisions builds the lush richness that can be created through the detail of your life together. The process starts anew with each decision.

A husband doesn't sweat the small stuff.

The opposite situation can be just as much of a problem. If one of you never seems to care very much about life's little stuff, the other can feel stuck with responsibility for deciding. In *The New Male,* Herb Goldberg claims this "actor-reactor" dynamic is at the root of much marital suffering. One party (often the husband) is expected to make all the decisions, to "act," while the wife "reacts," often by criticizing or suffering in silence over something she really did care about.

> Ault: *What shall we fix for the Krogmans for dinner tomorrow night?*
> Jean: *Chicken would be good.*
> Ault: *Well, we always have chicken, but I don't care.*
> Jean: *Well then, how about spaghetti?*
> Ault: *I guess so. That's kind of boring, though.*
> Jean: *We could send out for pizza.*
> Ault: *Okay, if you don't think they'll be disappointed.*

If a scenario like this recurs frequently, both husband and wife will feel frustration at trying to decide the small stuff of life. Too much is buried between the lines.

As another twist on this, sometimes neither of you will care very much. What to do? Try having a Decider of the Month. The DOM's job is to decide all those small details about which neither of you has a strong opinion or leaning. Both have to agree which items fall into this category, but once you do, the Decider must then follow through, and the non-decider can't complain. Don't be surprised if the "I don't care" person hates the idea at first. It's an eye-opener to realize how much power is buried in seeming not to care, but still criticizing.

Both of you need to take responsibility for decisions.

And finally, if the opposite holds, that is, you both feel strong energy and each of you wants to win, either find a way to compromise (see the chapter on Negotiating) or move on to the next chapter, Deciding Big Stuff.

A husband cares about life in all its detailed glory.

12

Deciding Big Stuff

Buying a house or car 　　　*Having children*
Moving to another town 　*Jobs & Money*
Caring for elderly parents

Big decisions represent a chance to shape your lives for the long-term future. Making them will be a lot easier if you're in general agreement about how you want that future to look. Issues such as those listed above may deeply affect both your lives, so deciding them must involve you both. When you guys decide on the big stuff in life, you're operating as a team. You're asking, "What's the best solution for the team?"

An underlying premise of Rule 1 (ASSUME YOU'RE TOGETHER FOR A PURPOSE) is *What's good for your marriage is also good for you.* It may be arduous to distinguish between doing what's best for your career or hers, and doing what's best for your marriage; but it's worth it. If the "best" job for you is in a city or profession that causes your family great hardship, it may not be so great for your marriage. Which priority is higher?

The days when a woman made blind sacrifices for the good of her husband's career are over. Blind is out. That doesn't mean she'll never decide to sacrifice something, but it does mean that both of you have to look at the question. You may be the one who has to give something up.

Big issues will arise in your marriage. When they do, use these steps for making joint decisions that serve your union:

1. **Look to your vision**. If you have created a Joint Vision Statement as suggested in Chapter 1, you've got a great start. Consider the big deci-

sion in the light of that vision. Will it further or hinder the things you have both said you most want out of life? Start by asking, *What solution will work best for our marriage?*

2. **Ask the deeper question.** *What experience are we seeking? What is it we are really* looking for, and what will *serve it?*
   Frequently, people confuse a potential means to a goal with the goal itself. For example, if the decision involves buying a big, fancy house, ask yourself why you are drawn to do so. If you are seeking to enjoy the fruits of your success and to provide room for your family to grow, the house may well provide a basis for that experience. But if you are seeking to feel more prosperous and to bring more harmony to your family, a low mortgage payment may be a better place to start. Either way, the house itself is just a prop. In other words, it may take additional ground-work for you to experience the satisfaction of prosperity or harmony. Decisions made after this type of reflection are much more likely to support you in choosing what you really want.

3. **Use logic.** Make lists of the pros and cons, the costs, the major consider-ations. Write them down. (If your wife wants to initiate the discussion and write the lists, then she should have that job. Otherwise, you do it. Husbands are men of action, remember?) Weigh the evidence. Compro-mise. Negotiate your differences.

4. **Use intuition.** Check your gut reaction and hers. Look for signs. (No kidding!) Psychiatrist Paul Pearsall has observed that his clients' major life choices are frequently facilitated by a meaningful coincidence. Call it your subconscious making up something, call it God, or call it the coin-cidence fairies—if you are open to your intuition, new forms of support become available. Trust these feelings. Women usually get most of the credit for intuition. With a little attention, yours can flourish, too.

   What if you can't tell the difference between your intuition and limiting emotions such as fear or vanity? Just ask yourself, *What else besides my intuition could be causing this "gut reaction"?* You'll know.

5. **Brainstorm.** When you're at an impasse, and it seems that none of the choices serve both you and your marriage, look for a creative new ap-proach. Make sure you both participate freely in the discussion. Write down all ideas, no matter how far-fetched. Consciously separate the think-ing part from the judging part. Later you get to decide which ideas have merit and which don't.
   If this process reveals that you genuinely don't want the same things out of life, then it may be time to face up to that. Perhaps one or both of you have changed. No amount of brainstorming will help if you want differ-ent things out of life and are unwilling to compromise.

6. **Decide**. Just do it. And then support it. When you do the best you can and trust things to work out, they usually do.

You'd have a pretty boring marriage if you both agreed on everything, but don't worry, you won't. You may even make a major decision together that you yourself are not wild about. You didn't want to agree, but you gave in. It happens. It does not, however, relieve you of your responsibility to endorse and support the decision once it's made.

In other words, get behind the decision. You made it as a team, and you're a co-equal partner of the team, sharing the responsibility for carrying out your team's decision. Do your part, and do it enthusiastically. It will serve your marriage.

A husband is a team player.

13

Decorating

Liz loved the notion of furnishing a home and creating a special space for the family. Steve felt neither the time nor the inclination to participate. Both were content that she shoulder the responsibility for feathering their nest. Everyone said the end result was warm, inviting, creative, and wholly Liz. As much fun as it was to be in their home, Steve's "presence" was absent. It was her home.

When two people join together in marriage, their tastes merge where they live. They assume that this mix will flow naturally and that their individual styles will integrate and blend harmoniously. It doesn't always work that way.

The stereotype husband has no interest in decorating; he leaves that to his wife. Indeed, if she enjoys decorating the home and does it better than you, why shouldn't she get the job? If, on the other hand, you care about color schemes, rugs, furniture, paintings, and all the rich detail of your home environment, you should be involved.

But there's more at stake than just how your house looks. Establishing your environment is a means of expressing yourself as part of the team. Since you're co-equal partners in this adventure of playing house, participate in it. It's a way to ensure that both of your creative energies contribute to the place you live in. Don't fall into the trap of conceding that one of you is the "artistic" one and thus should decide all things creative. That thinking lets the other one off the hook for all imaginative activities. In other words, even if you're neither good at nor thrilled by the prospect of beautifying or adorning your living space, find some way to contribute.

Eventually, Steve started a small workshop in the basement, requiring that he "decorate" a space. In this case, the job meant choosing functional lighting, practical storage, useful tools, and a pleasant work space. It wasn't what company saw when they visited the living room, but at least his energy infused part of their home.

You can do at least as well as Steve. Stake a claim to some aspect of your home environment.

As with so much of living together, arbitration and concessions help. If both of you have strong feelings about how your home should look, compromise. Give her one room and you take another. If you want to display all your photographs in the den and she prefers a spare look, find a way; don't slough it off. Tell her what's in it for you (pride, reminiscence, etc.) and where you'll concede on other points.

For functional items, the one affected most should hold sway. She wants a home computer for her work; the best lighting for it is the den. You want that room to relax in. You want a pet entrance in the back door for your dog. She doesn't like the idea, but it will save steps and energy. She gets the PC and you get the dog door.

Just for fun sometime, you might ask yourself how your tastes and attitudes toward decorating reflect your personalities. Most people's do. Perhaps her preference for a formal living room bespeaks her respect for tradition, while your preference for a modern look comes from your openness to new ideas. Decorating your home takes on a whole new perspective when you become conscious that it's a way to show others who you are.

A husband wants to create the best environment for his marriage to flourish. Put some of your personal energy into that environment by infusing your home with some of your personality. Help decorate it.

A husband contributes something of himself to his home.

14

Dressing

- *I have to look at you more than you have to look at yourself, so why won't you wear something I like for a change?*
- *You may be right, but I don't feel good in those styles, and that's what matters: How I feel in them.*
- *Okay, but how about stretching a little? Wear this and see how it feels. Blue looks good on you. Humor me.*
- *How would you like it if I told you what to wear?*
- *I probably wouldn't. What did you have in mind?*

Sound familiar? Many of us play some variation of this tune from time to time. Both these people have valid points. Recommending that your spouse wear something to please you seems a reasonable request. So does wanting to feel right in clothes, to feel appropriately dressed, or at least not to feel silly or uncomfortable.

Dressing is a means of self-expression. A man who dresses GQ and one who dresses as though it doesn't matter what he has on are both making a statement. A statement of individuality.

So what does this have to do with being a husband?

Taking a dressing cue from her is one small way to say, "You matter most to me." If she wants to see you in a certain shirt or tie or thinks it's sexy when you wear your black shorts, do it—unless you feel really inappropriate. Don't make a big deal out of it. Perhaps she has a more tuned in sense of color and style than you. If not, you're doing it just to please her. That's not so bad. You're still the one choosing whether to go along or not.

Notice what she wears. She chooses it partly to look good for you and wants to know what pleases you. If she asks you what she should wear to dinner at your aunt's (whom she's never met) or to your company's office party, don't beg off; find out and tell her. She needs your input on what's appropriate and on what you'd like to see her in.

Tell her what you like in clothes for yourself, including sizes, so she'll be able to buy presents. Keep a list of her sizes. Notice the styles, colors, materials she likes and looks good in. If these activities seem insignificant, realize their cumulative import. Little things add up.

A husband is involved (even if only slightly) in what his wife wears, and he lets her be involved in what he wears. It's one of the many small ways he stays close to her. It takes very little time, yet helps weave the fabric of intimacy that keeps love alive.

A husband uses every opportunity to say I love you.

CHAPTER

15

Drying Her Tears

She cries when she's happy and she cries when she's sad, and I can't always tell the difference. Besides, I never know what to do about it.

Maybe you don't have to do anything. Or maybe you do. What's the appropriate response when your wife begins sobbing?

Here are some possibilities:

She cries when she's happy.

Smile and realize that you have nothing to do with these particular tears. They're not about you; they're about her and how she expresses joy. You don't have to respond. Just share the joy with her.

Women seem to do more of this kind of crying than men. But know that tears of laughter and happiness can lift and exhilarate anyone, and no one need apologize for such open release of emotion. Weddings and births and specially chosen gifts often move husbands and wives to happy crying.

She cries when she's sad.

Hold her. Tell her you know she's sad. Tell her that everything is going to be all right. Even if you don't believe that everything is going to be all right, at that moment she needs to be reassured that the world is safe and that you're there for her. It's one of the best parts of your job as husband.

She cries when she's mad at you.

Don't get mad back. Her tears are manifestations of a strong emotion; she's angry, and crying is the way she's expressing that feeling. It's like sadness. Acknowledge the anger but deal only with the sorrow until the tears dry. Then see the chapter on Fighting.

45

She cries for no apparent reason.

Take a moment to assess what's going on. You know she's not crying for the first three reasons—happy, sad, or angry. *It's something I don't understand. Maybe she doesn't either.*

In the middle of an argument or discussion, your wife begins to cry, and you haven't a clue what's going on. Sometimes she doesn't either and just writes it off to hormones. But whether she understands them or not, her emotions have taken over at this moment and she can't continue using both her mind and body. For the time being, the body has won, and all it wants to do is cry.

Tell her you know she's affected strongly and that you can return to the conversation (or whatever you were doing) later when she's better able. Think of it as an unexpected time out.

There's no need to mention your confusion over her behavior. She knows that these particular tears are irrational. Making it seem as though she just did something "to you" will only make it worse. Some things we don't understand; we just accept.

The condition is temporary. She'll get past it, and you both know it. The idea here is that while you—the responsible man of action—want to do something or say something so that you can get back to normal, you can't. At least not at this moment. She's incapacitated. Trying to continue as though nothing was happening or getting mad or trying to get her to stop crying will be counterproductive, and you'll just frustrate the both of you. Asking her to explain what she's crying about doesn't work either.

A husband dries tears with strong, quiet understanding and acceptance.

CHAPTER

16

Eating

Not so strange a topic for a husband's manual after you take a closer look. Take a minute, and name the three different sensual activities you enjoy most.

If eating is one of them, you're lucky; you get to do it several times a day. And when you're a husband, you get to do it with your wife. What could be better?

There is probably no romantic image with more universal appeal than that of a candlelit dinner for two. You know the scene: flowers, a sense of expectation, a well-set table, specially chosen foods, attentiveness to your dinner companion, and oh, that candlelight! Married people have the opportunity to bring some or all of these features to every meal. Even with children, rituals can be established that say eating is a special time. And when you have no time or energy for any of this, a simple moment to look quietly into her eyes as the meal begins can say, "This is special to me. I appreciate our life together."

Think of the many metaphors of eating and your life with her: providing sustenance for your family, breaking bread together, sharing in the fruits of your labor, blessing your bounty before a meal.

A husband who also prepares food even gets a chance to add some love to the other ingredients. Certainly, not all husbands should become cooks, but all husbands will benefit from eating as part of celebrating life.

You go through a lot of daily rituals with this woman, and along with sleeping, this may be the one you do most often. Why not make eating with her into something more, something to serve your marriage.

- Fix meals she especially enjoys, and appreciate the ones she fixes especially for you.
- Make toasts.

- Find a moment at each meal to honor her.
- Turn this daily activity into an intimate sharing.

A husband celebrates life.

17

Expressing Your Feelings

What an unemotional jerk she's married to; he's so distant and detached!
What an overly sensitive baby she married; he gets upset at every little thing.

Which strikes you as the worse insult?

Both emotional extremes, the seemingly heartless tough guy and the high-strung, fragile type are frowned on in our society. One for being uninvolved with his emotions, the other for being ruled by them. The key is to find a balance: Acknowledge whatever feelings you have, and let them out appropriately.

You and your wife are a team, and you don't want your teammate to operate in the dark about you; you want her to know your feelings. They're as important as your thoughts. On the other hand, you don't want to overdo it and lose control of your emotions. After all, you are in charge of how you respond to your emotions. In order to assume this full control, however, you must first acknowledge them to yourself. Denying them or trying to hide them eventually leads to a dam bursting, one way or another. Finding a balance may require some difficult inner work, but you're up to it.

Rule 1 recommends complete honesty, especially with yourself. Start by recognizing and accepting your feelings. No matter where they originated, any feelings you have are legitimate and yours. No one (including your wife) *made* you feel a certain way; you just feel the way you feel. Instead of backing away from feelings or pretending you don't know what they are, welcome them as a part of you, and tell your wife about them. Don't judge them and don't allow her to judge you for having them.

Obviously, you don't have to act on any given emotion, but denying that you ever had the feelings in the first place is not in your best interests—or hers. Expressing your feelings doesn't mean flying into a rage when you feel anger or weeping uncontrollably every time you're sad. It means finding some way to declare or recognize what's going on; it means sharing more of you with your wife.

I'm feeling jealous right now.

I'm uncomfortable around those people.

I feel crowded and not in control whenever that happens.

I feel like crying.

If you absolutely can't bring yourself to say the words, try sound effects. Really. A good growl or even a baby-like "Wanh!" can let your wife in on what you are feeling while maybe even adding a little comic relief. Let those feelings out!

During the Persian Gulf War, General Norman Schwartzkopf said, "Any man who doesn't cry scares me." He understood the value of tears. Tears have been proven to release toxic chemicals from the body that build up under stress. Crying can benefit you physically and emotionally. It can also clean the slate so that you can turn the corner and be ready to accept the next joy. Why hold back? Do you really believe that men aren't supposed to cry?

Find some way to express the emotions that have the strongest impact on you; the harder it is to communicate, the more important that you find a suitable way. Tell her when you're happy, when you're proud, when you're nervous or uncertain. As Garth Brooks asks, "If tomorrow never comes, will she know how much I love her?" Tell her. Often. Expressing your feelings does not prevent you from being a strong, responsible man of action; on the contrary, it helps. You are finding a balance that will serve both you and your marriage.

And remember, she is not *making* you feel anything; *you* own your emotions. The best way to take complete ownership is to start with your language. This is another opportunity to use "I" statements, which help you keep the focus on you (where it belongs). Compare these two statements:

(a) *You're driving me nuts over this picnic at your mother's. Do we have to go?*

(b) *I don't know. I'm a little uneasy about attending your mother's picnic this Fourth of July.*

Statement (a) might sound more natural, but it removes you from the problem; it's your wife's fault (she's making you crazy). You ask a rhetorical question which actually reflects your own indecision. Statement (b) doesn't solve the problem of whether to attend the picnic, but it puts the issue where it belongs—with you. You are the one with the mixed emotions, so comment on it, acknowledge it. Now you can put your energy into solving the problem (whether to attend the picnic) rather than into covering up your feelings.

As a last resort, at least be willing to admit to her that it's hard for you to express your feelings about something. Just saying that can prevent her from assuming that you don't have any.

If you're thinking, "People don't talk this way in real life," think again. People whose lives are enriched by their marriage, whose self-assuredness is based on honest and reflective communication seem to have deeper, happier lives. They probably stay married longer, too.

A husband expresses his feelings appropriately.

18

Fighting

If you find yourself winning an argument with your wife,
apologize immediately.
(suggested by the world's oldest human being in Robert Heinlein's *Time Enough for Love*)

This humorous gem of advice acknowledges that winning a battle sometimes means losing the war.

When disputes arise, we often have a lot invested in our point of view, so we join the battle. Instead of negotiating calmly, we fight. No one ever admits it, but a part of us enjoys the contest; it feels important that we win. Sometimes we use tactics and strategies that win fights but damage our long-term relationships. In other words, sometimes we do things that don't serve our marriage. There are, however, ways to avoid such miscalculations. Here's how:

1. **No hitting**. Ever. Dispel any myths you have about the occasional need for physical force; it's an outdated notion. And it sets in motion resentments and fears which exhaust the spirit of your marriage. Find another expression for your emotions. Give them voice.
   I'm starting to lose control. I'm angry enough to hit something. I need to run or work out or scream. I need a break.

2. **Stay focused**. As soon as your emotions get high, stop and think: What's the central issue here? Let's stick to it. Staying on the point prevents venturing into previous hurts. Don't bring up the past unless it's directly relevant. If she brings up something off the point, address it briefly, then get back on target.
   Yes, I know I blew it last month when I forgot that phone call. If you'd like, we can talk about that next. But for now, let's keep to this subject.

3. **Mentally step back**. Do a split-second reality check. Is there something else going on? If you're fighting for the excitement of battle, stop and see if it's worth it.
   No, wait. This is going nowhere fast. Let's regroup.

4. **Go to the well within**. It never runs dry. The wellspring of you is an inner core that cannot be hurt; it's a never-ending source of strength and good will. Tap it whenever you feel beaten down by the latest fight. Meditate, pray, walk around the block, whatever. It'll always provide you with new energy, and perhaps a way to resolve the problem.
   I am still. There is a place within me that is safe and loving.

5. **Redirect your energy toward something positive**. Turn the fight into a negotiation in which your goal is to resolve differences. (See the chapter on Negotiating.) There are no losers in successful mediation, only winners.
   I don't want to bully or be bullied, or even hold a grudge. I want the best for our marriage. Let's come at this from another direction.

6. **Move on**. If you've done something you regret, acknowledge it, apologize if appropriate, resolve openly to improve, and forgive yourself. Be genuine and sincere. You can always make a fresh start.

7. **Reach for higher ground**. Find something positive to learn from this fight. If it recurs regularly, it could be with you a lifetime. Solving it could be the key to a much improved marriage. Review the New Rules (Chapter 1), and use every tool you have to serve this higher goal.

A husband fights fair.

19

Getting Along

It's not always easy to get along with people, particularly the ones you live with. Just ask your wife.

The best way to get along is to start with a robust, clear-cut intent to be positive. A congenial, good-natured husband creates an atmosphere of harmony in his marriage. He sees that good will serves his relationship and in no way endangers his free will. He's still free to disagree and to let his dissent be known. He simply does so harmoniously.

The major key is to recognize the difference between reaction and response. First you react to something, then you respond. Reacting is the one you have less control over. You startle at an unexpected, loud noise. You blink when an object suddenly nears your eye. You wince at the possibility of her mother's visit. You react.

When you react to something your wife says or does, remember that's only the first part. And as a rule, an inner one. The next part, the one you can always control, is your response. You investigate the noise and perhaps fix it. You move away from objects that put your eye at risk. You talk to her about the length of the visit. You respond.

Allow time between reacting and responding. In between, think. If you are upset, this may mean walking around the block while you cool off. You are creating a chance to figure out how you really feel and what you want to do about it. The way you respond when you come back is the way you get along with her. Wait until you can create an atmosphere of trust and ease in your communication.

If you find yourself picking on her or being generally unpleasant, stop it. No matter what she says or does (even if she feels cranky and just wants to bitch), you're the only one in charge of you. Choose responses that will serve your marriage. Even if you grew up in a home which was a constant battleground, you can choose to get along.

If she gets irritable and harps at you, don't be combative. Work at being understanding and kind. Go out of your way to respond pleasantly and lovingly, and do so from a position of strength and self-assuredness. Point out what you think is going on and ask her to join you in creating accord. If this sounds like a tall order, it is. Your naturally combative instincts may be put to a severe test at times. But what's the alternative, an escalation of hostilities? What will that get you?

Getting along serves both you and your marriage, and it's more important than winning an argument or getting angry, even if you feel it was her "fault."

A husband gets along with his wife.

20

Getting Help

It's easier to be a prince when you're married to a princess.

But what if you're not? Some women have deeply imbedded patterns of self-destructive behavior, just as some men do. Your wife may have problems with roots stemming back long before you met that block your learning and growing together. If you or she (or the two of you together) experiences repeated behavior that harms your relationship, it's time to think about getting help.

Rule 1 reminds you to use everything in life for your learning. If you are going to do this, you'll probably need some help occasionally. We all do. The Best Seller's List is chock full of terrific self-help books. Read a few. Libraries and bookstores are valuable resources. Urge your wife to read the same books, and discuss them with her. If this seems awkward, join a group that discusses such books, or start one yourself. Churches, temples, and psychologically and spiritually oriented local organizations often have book discussion clubs.

Those same organizations also sponsor couples workshops, intensive weekends, and intimacy seminars. These are not just for people with troubled marriages. Think of them as refresher courses, as ways to keep up with the latest changes. (And there will always be changes; that's the one immutable law of life.)

If you're looking for support, don't overlook the new men's organizations that are springing up around the country. There's more to them than you might have heard. Many men who believed that the only male bonding ritual they needed required a ballgame and a six-pack have been surprised at their satisfaction in rediscovering the best of their male heritage through these groups. And being in touch with the best of your manhood will definitely serve your marriage.

Besides being refreshers, these approaches can also be helpful if your marriage isn't all you want it to be. There's nothing wrong with getting a little help. Learning and growing together is an excellent way to keep love alive.

In cases where the love is almost dead, getting help may be a more immediate and serious matter. Working with a therapist or marriage counselor may seem like a last resort, but sometimes that's what it takes. Remember the joke about the farmer who wanted to treat his mule gently but kept a 2-by-4 handy to make sure he got its attention? Sometimes life has to smack us upside the head to get us to notice a problem. When it does, there's always a positive way to respond to it. Seeking help is one of those ways.

Rule 1 reminds us that a husband and wife are together for a purpose. That purpose is usually to learn something and to grow a little—or a lot. In finding out what this purpose is, don't fall into the trap of wasting time on guilt or regret. Feeling sorry for himself gets in the way of a husband's being a strong and responsible man of action. He seeks to learn and grow and to help his wife do the same.

A husband is not afraid to ask for help.

21

Giving, Giving in, & Forgiving

Nobody likes giving in. It's rarely a positive stance. Even the words have an air of defeat about them. *Giving in.* It usually feels like defeat, as though you are giving up a part of yourself.

Giving, on the other hand, means coming from a position of strength. Sometimes the difference may be just a matter of a split-second's attitude adjustment.

> *Ron: Okay, okay, you win. I quit. I'm tired of fighting; we'll do it your way.*
> *Ana: You don't sound very happy about it.*
> *Ron: I'm ecstatic. (He hears the sarcasm in his own voice.) No, it's okay. Really.*
>   *I'll make the best of it.*

Look at the dialogue dispassionately; notice the shift Ron makes. His original surrender includes a disguised attack, but a moment later he has genuinely "come around." He has turned *giving in* into *giving.*

Here's a way you can do the same:

First, set priorities. How important is this matter to you? What's the cost to your individuality or to your marriage? (See the chapters "Negotiating" and "Fighting.") When it *is* important, stick to your guns. If you feel intense about something after you've considered it carefully, hold your ground, especially on issues that dramatically affect your life (whether and when to have children, for example). In other words, if it's not just stubborn pride, if you are committed to a behavior, a belief, or a course of action, and have decided to stand fast, then do it. You won't feel good about yourself long if you don't maintain your values. Being a giving husband doesn't mean giving in all the time. You can always agree to disagree.

On the other hand, many (perhaps most) issues you argue over truly aren't worth the cost of victory. It just makes sense to give in. Now the shift: *Giving in* becomes *giving* when you redirect your energies to something positive.

So, get with the program. On those occasions when you are resigned to "losing," turn that energy around; flip it. Release your tension (drop your shoulders and take a deep breath); then instead of seeing your wife as taking something from you, visualize yourself as offering something to her.

You'll be amazed at how much difference this subtle shift can make. So will she. You'll "win a few and lose a few," and in each instance you'll serve your marriage best by fully supporting the final outcome. No grudges. Let go of resentments or bitterness.

Chuck didn't want to add on to the house; Kimberly did. Even though he had misgivings, he decided to give in. His strong inclination was to go along sullenly but continue to grumble about the cost and inconvenience. Instead, he "got it." He understood that this would drain valuable energy from their relationship. He set up camp for them in the basement and suggested a fancy dinner out during the worst of the construction. He made the best of it.

Once you decide, it's a waste of energy to feel "stuck" with the outcome; you are now a part of it. Enthusiastically support the consequences. As a marriage-enhancing technique, this approach works, even when you still think she's "wrong."

A husband knows when and how to turn *giving in* into *giving*.

• • •

This *giving* to her can take many forms. Rub her feet, for example. A sure winner. If you're a giving type of guy, you probably already do. You like making her feel good and being considerate of her needs. You know she appreciates how you look out for her. You feel good about yourself. It's the best.

If you're not a naturally giving man, it won't be the best, but you can learn. Remember that you and your wife are together for a reason. Maybe this is it—to learn to become a giving person. If so, she's your best teacher.

Norman Vincent Peale used to advise those with low self-esteem to "fake it 'til you make it," to feign confidence, acting the way poised people do along the path toward self-assuredness. Good advice here, too. You know what considerate, giving husbands do. Copy them. Pretend you're kind by doing kind things for your wife on your way to becoming a giving husband.

Remember, too, the words of the poet Kahlil Gibran so often quoted at weddings: "You give but little when you give of your possessions. It is when you give of yourself that you truly give."

A husband is a giving man.

• • •

And probably the highest form of giving is forgiving.

To err is human; to forgive, divine. It's no accident that this wonderful expression describes forgiveness as a holy endeavor. It's a cardinal lesson of life—and the hardest—especially when it comes to forgiving yourself. Once again, your wife is your best teacher. As with so many other bits of advice in this manual, forget the hypothetical, and look to the practical. Learning forgiveness serves your marriage; punishing someone or holding on to resentments does not.

Often, troubled marriages end because this lesson remains unlearned. Know how important forgiveness is to your marriage. This doesn't mean being a passive punching bag. You don't have to accept abusive behavior patterns she may exhibit—work to remedy them. However, at the same time, know that whether her offenses were major or minor, forgiveness is a necessary first step for the return of intimacy. It serves you as much as it serves her.

The key is letting go. As a strong, responsible man of action, you are in control of your choices in life. You can choose to let go of anything that does not serve your marriage. Jealousy and resentment, for example, are fears that do not serve you in any way. Along with other fears you carry around, they get in the way of a marriage you can take pride in and feel good about. Let go of them.

A husband is a giving and forgiving man.

22

Giving Presents

Secretly, husbands are kids at heart. In fact, most people *love* getting presents. Oh, we may try to hide it. And after a lifetime of ill-considered or well-meaning but off-the-mark gifts, many of us have trained ourselves not to get too excited. But there's no one who's heart doesn't skip a small beat at the sight of a beribboned package or at the words, "I've brought home a surprise for you." Giving gifts is one of the easiest ways to keep fun in your marriage. It's especially delightful when you learn to give and receive gifts thoughtfully.

Mal wanted a set of drill bits for his birthday, but Kristin got him a tie. Bummer, he thought. I won't say anything now, but she should have known. Besides, this tie is gross.

We seem genuinely surprised all our lives that other people don't think the way we do. Well, they don't. Where presents are concerned, one side of your job is to let your wife know what you want. Sure, presents are supposed to be surprises, but the best part of any present is the thought behind it—the saying is true. Assume that she enjoys doing things for you, giving you presents, pleasing you. Help her by dropping hints or telling her outright what's on your Wish List.

If your wife is Kristin, if she can't read your mind, if she seems not to pay attention to your signals, be straightforward. Tell her outright. You'll both be better off. And when she does get you something, say Thank you. Forget that old business of telling her she shouldn't have. Just show sincere appreciation. (Of course she should have!)

A husband receives gifts graciously.

The other side of your job is to find out what things she wants, and then remember to give them to her. Look for clues (an author she has just begun reading), listen for hints (complaints about old gloves), or ask her (or friends or relatives) outright. Once in a while be daring and try something completely new (a flashy outfit or a session with a fashion photographer).

Of course your home will always need new or replacement items, such as a coffee pot, a screwdriver, or towels. All valid choices as gifts, you might reason. True, *if* you both decide it's okay, and if you don't do it all the time. Be open with her about whether you'd like certain gift-giving occasions to be house-related or personal. Listen to her wishes, too.

Lyn would love it if John "cared" enough to know what she wanted for her birthday, including size, color, and style. Perhaps she has even dropped hints about wanting some special clay for her potter's wheel. For his part, John has been swamped with work at the office and barely has time to get a card. He gets her steak knives.

Are you ever John? Sometimes the stuff of life nudges out other priorities, and the tendency is to buy candy or something requiring little thought. Find the time. If it's important to her, it's important. Plan ahead. You know when presents are expected, and you know what she likes. Put it on your calendar and follow through. Remember, this is the love of your life.

• • •

The other half of this equation is giving gifts to others. Gifts for your children, your friends, and your family are joint ventures. (Remember, it's all one family, now!) You may be more qualified to suggest presents for certain people. When that's true, don't shy away from it. It's part of your responsibility. Urge her to participate similarly.

When you give presents as a couple, you both share the responsibility, so don't usurp it or ignore it. Responsibility doesn't imply the actual purchasing of gifts. Who has more time? More inclination? More taste and patience? Use your head. Work it out with her as to who goes to the store or sends the card or calls in the order or wraps the present.

If you really hate doing this, tell her how you feel and negotiate the task. Don't ignore it; it won't go away. A wife who resignedly picks up a disregarded job often resents it. And that doesn't serve your marriage. If you *really, really* hate doing this, ask yourself why. See the chapter "Taking a Closer Look."

If she's in charge of choosing, buying, and wrapping gifts, make sure you know what's in them. They're from both of you, so don't be in the dark. Don't reinforce the stereotype of a bumbling husband whose only home skills are eating and changing the oil. A husband is involved in the goings-on of the family.

Give unselfishly and give often: big stuff, little stuff, silly stuff.

A husband gives gifts generously and thoughtfully.

23

Going Public

Gina: I hate it when you correct my grammar in public.

Bill: Don't be so sensitive. You don't want people to think you're ignorant, do you?

Gina: I'm not ignorant. I just don't care as much about form as you do, but that's not my point. I don't want people to see us at odds with each other; we're a couple—a team. We should act that way.

Bill: What if you make a factual error, like saying Oregon is on the East Coast?

Gina: That's different, but even then you don't have to embarrass me. You're my husband not my school teacher.

You may want to make a distinction between how you treat each other in public and how you handle a situation when you're alone. The chapters "Having it Both Ways" and "Supporting" both address the issue of you as an individual versus you as a couple, that is, "you" as both a singular and a plural pronoun. Playing this out in public adds an additional, sometimes intricate, dimension. It certainly will require your attention; you are no longer just "you," you are also "you two."

Here's a rule of thumb:

Present a united front whenever it doesn't compromise your personal code of morality or ethics. A temporary silence may be better for your marriage than a public contradiction or squabbling. Disagreements are natural and healthy, but timing is still everything.

Of course, if it's a spirited discussion of politics, movie stars, or the meaning of life, don't hold back. Being a publicly agreeable couple doesn't mean denying your opinions. It means being thoughtful, thinking before you open your mouth, and respecting your wife's wishes.

If she's not comfortable with public disagreements, or if it's a serious matter, tell her privately. Her feelings are much more important than your need to be right or to prove her illogical or wrong.

Perhaps you're the one who's sensitive to this issue. Talk it over with your wife; find out where you both draw the line at the public airing of differences. She may need help in adjusting to your ways, so let her know how you feel. Lay it out for her—your expectations, your reasons, your goals. Don't wait until something upsetting happens and then overreact.

It's never okay to try to get others to side with you against your mate or to publicly chastise her; you're her partner, not her owner or trainer. There may be times, however, when it's appropriate to refer to serious differences, especially if you can do so with a genuine intent to get help from friends or to support others with similar problems.

Sally and I have had a real go-round about how much we run up on our credit cards. Jeff, how do you and Merrianne handle money problems?

Even in this instance, however, it's best that you both agree that asking Jeff and Merrianne for input is okay. Don't decide on your own.

A husband presents a united front with his wife.

24

Growing Old Together

Will you still need me, will you still feed me,
When I'm sixty-four?

Paul McCartney & John Lennon

If you are truly going to grow old with this woman, it wouldn't hurt to think about what growing old means. Among other things, it means changes: all that mid-life crisis business, her menopause, gravity, the empty-nest, perhaps grandparenting, a quieter energy in your relationship. She'll change and so will you.

Unfortunately, when most of us think of aging we worry about the worst case scenario instead of planning for the best case.

Wife   *Growing old scares me.*

Husband *I think what we're building now will enhance our passages into old age; I know it can. I assume we can be fully alive and even get better and better.*

Wife   *Sounds a little Pollyanna. Look at that elderly couple next door; they never talk to each other, even at meals. There's no life in their marriage.*

Husband *That doesn't have to happen to us. Changes will come in our relationship, but they don't have to be all bad ones. Plus, you've got me by your side to share in the challenge.*

Wife   *I hate the idea of being sick and old and not able to take care of myself.*

Husband *Me too. I want to believe that growing old will be gentle and friendly for us and not so hard to accept.*

You can grow old happy. Start now by holding an image of graceful aging as part of your joint vision. Envision your role as husband continuing through the changes, still a strong, responsible man of action. Program it.

If you're smart, you are working on a long-term financial plan, saving and investing now for your future together. But how are you doing on your long-term emotional plan? Can you envision the two of you facing the aging process together with grace and joy?

Maybe you've already thought about where you'd like to retire. But have you thought about the habits, skills, and attitudes you'll need in order to enjoy that place together? Plan ahead. Visualize what it will be like. Talk to her about it—even the hard parts—infirmity, fears of boredom or isolation, even death. The best preparation is confidence in your love and in the ability each of you has to tap into your inner resources.

If many of the other suggestions in this book sound too hard or not worth the effort, think of them as long-term investments. You're building your emotional and spiritual nest egg for the years ahead.

The notion that life can be more harmonious as you age sounds like "pie in the sky," especially when things are tough or when an illness occurs. Harmony comes when the relationship has been built on trust and personal responsibility. Practice the principles outlined in this book, and fight only the important battles. Take care of the little things so the big things (like relying on each other) can come naturally.

Infirmities and financial insecurity tend to push people toward the edge. It gets pretty scary when you feel your mortality or worry about the next paycheck. Remember the prime directive. It's not an accident that you are facing these problems together. Rely on her. Share your strengths and use the problems of life as opportunities for growth, both personal and marital.

In more primitive times, our ancestral parents huddled together at night to protect and comfort each other from the cold and dark. We still have each other to help face unknown fears of health and economic uncertainty.

A husband helps his wife grow old. He's there to help her, to hold her hand. He accepts the same help from her.

25

Having Friends

Pat has friends from work, through her church group, and some she grew up with. She enjoys spending time with them, and they love her. Gary doesn't care for many of them. His friends are mostly from the softball team, the Rotarians, and his old high school. His best friends are single. Pat doesn't dislike them; she just doesn't have much in common with them or their wives or girl friends.

Chances are you came into this marriage with your own set of friends, some of them ex-girl friends or lovers. So did she. Some of these friends will naturally drift away as you become a new person within your marriage. With a little effort, many of the rest will become friends to you both. But what about those who don't? Is it okay for you to maintain separate friends?

Rule 3 reminds you to take responsibility for your own happiness. She's responsible for her own happiness, too. If, like Gary, you'd rather be around your friends than hers, that's up to you. Obviously, you want to strike a balance of time with your separate and mutual friends and time together as a couple. There's no innate reason why old loyalties have to interfere with new ones, and vice versa.

Talk about it; it's worth the effort to try. Can you integrate sets of friends? Be realistic. How much time do you need with old pals? Obviously, ex-lovers are a special case. Don't even think of arguing that they're just like other friends now. But every case is different. Balance is the key, and there's no set balance that works for all couples.

When children are involved, it is obviously in a husband's (or wife's) best interest to be on good terms with an ex-spouse. Friendship, however, is not always possible. Bring an extra measure of trust and sensitivity to this one, but don't fake it. If you're uncomfortable, say so.

Separate friends can also be fertile grounds for trouble when they come to represent something about your spouse that you don't like. Our friends reflect pieces of who we are. Is there some part of her you wish she'd left behind when you married her? Is there some part of you you're ready to leave behind, perhaps along with some old drinking buddies from your "wild" days? Your friends represent a chance for each of you to open new doors or close old ones when appropriate.

Take care about making unilateral decisions about your time. When accepting an invitation to do something on your own, ask her permission—even if it's pro forma or after the fact. *Honey, I told Walt I'd go golfing with him on Saturday. Is that all right?* This acknowledges the fact that your relationship with her comes first, and if she's insecure, it gives her some sense of control. (It also establishes a model of how you'd like to be treated by her.)

Of course, if she always says no, you've got some work to do. There may be some hidden lessons here. If she always seems irritated at the amount of time you spend with friends or at how they influence you, consider it. Is she on to something? Are you hanging on to some part of your past that no longer serves you or using others to put some distance between you and your wife? Even if you're not doing it consciously, you may be tapping into some fears of desertion or abandonment she may have. Everyone is a little scared and lonely.

On the other hand, if you always object to her spending time with friends, check your motives. Do you genuinely feel you're not getting as much of her time as you need, or do you feel threatened by her friends or activities? If you consistently end up peeved at your wife's friends and then make her side with you out of loyalty, step back and wonder. Perhaps there's some hard-to-admit fear of abandonment you are carrying around. This is one of the deepest kinds of challenges a marriage can face. Good thing you're up to it.

Work together to resolve these dilemmas. It's a great opportunity to get past some touchy stuff or negative qualities (groundless jealousy, possessiveness, free-floating fears, judgments). The reward for getting past them is the extra richness a variety of friends can bring to your individual lives and thus to your marriage.

A husband is both a loyal friend AND a supportive part of the marriage team.

26

Having It Both Ways:
Being your own man and hers, too

Rule 1: Assume you're together for a purpose

Rule 2: Honor your differences

These two rules may appear to be in conflict. How can you reconcile them? How can you have both intimacy and autonomy?

George: What do you guys think about the new school board candidate?

Laurie: Zach, what do we think?

Zach: We like him; that is, I like him. Why don't you read the papers and decide for yourself.

Laurie: Well, I usually agree with your judgment.

Zach: Not in the last election, you didn't. You even campaigned for that character from upstate.

Laurie: Well, that was different; we agreed to disagree.

People treat you differently when you're part of a couple. Single people are clearly "one." Married people are sort of "one" and yet still "two." You still need to pay two shares of any joint bill with others and two fares on an airline, but invitations and presents often assume you are one unit. Sometimes people even assume you have similar opinions. You get confused, too. How much independence, how much interdependence? How can I "be my own man" if I focus so much on being her husband? Can I have it both ways? This may be the most difficult set of adjustments a husband has to make. It plays itself out in many areas of your life, as reflected in the chapters Having Friends, Sharing Interests, Supporting, and Going Public (as a couple).

69

Bookstores are filled with useful advice on dealing with co-dependence, a relationship that often shows up as one partner acting overly dependent while the other acts overly autonomous. Here's a way to boil down that advice into a simple formula:

$$1 + 1 = 3$$

One whole, strong person plus another whole, strong person can make a marriage that exceeds the sum of their separate contributions. But only if the partners use their separate strengths to work for the good of the whole, surrendering their own needs when necessary. It's a paradox, all right. The basic premise of this book is what's good for the relationship is also good for you. But that never means giving up who you are for the good of your wife. You may have to let go of some behaviors or attitudes that aren't serving your marriage, but that doesn't affect who you are. The goal is to have two confident people co-creating a dynamic marriage.

Where you started out will determine whether you need to strengthen your individuality and autonomy or your ability to be intimate and interdependent. If you were a long-time playboy, a captain of industry, or a free-thinking, creative, independent type, chances are your marriage will benefit as you learn to depend more on her. But if your wife has more confidence, money, power, success, or education, strengthening your own individuality may contribute best to the formula of two strong equals.

Regardless of where you start, these tips can help you move toward a point of balance:

- Develop your own skills, tastes, and strengths in order to be the most fully alive person you can be, and encourage her to do the same. Remember that you're responsible for your own happiness, as is your wife.
- When there's an apparent conflict between your needs and those of your union, give all you can, but don't give up who you are. Of course, you will also always be open to expanding your definition of who you are.
- Don't sweat the publicly accepted symbols of union. Shared opinions or joint presents and invitations are indeed symbols of oneness, but they don't deny your individuality. You should be able to state opinions or give presents jointly or singly as an occasion warrants without having to make it a statement of your unity or individuality. In other words, don't let others' behaviors or reactions determine your attitude. You know where you end and she begins.
- Develop pride in her—not just in her accomplishments or looks, but in her whole being. You are retaining your individuality, but part of you is part of her. When people view you two, they see reflections of one on the other, whether you like it or not. Be proud to be married to her.
- Develop an equally strong sense of pride in your union. Your team is making its own special mark on the world.

A husband is his own man and his wife's man, too.

27

Housekeeping
or
The Art of Compromise

- *Right now, I'm being the breadwinner, and you're the homemaker. To me that includes housekeeping.*
- *I don't mind doing most of the work, but it wouldn't hurt you to clean a toilet once in a while.*
- *When I come home from work, I want to relax, not do some of your work.*
- *Well, the least you can do is take out the garbage.*

What is this, some kind of contest?

Let's face it guys, no matter how up to date a man considers himself, there's still a little voice way down inside that says housework is women's work. Even if she's out working a longer day than you are, do you ever catch yourself doing the laundry but not taking it out of the dryer? Buying groceries but not putting them away? Or washing the dishes except for that one greasy pot? You know the syndrome: the subconscious belief that some magic force is going to come along and finish the job. Well, there is no magic. You're going to have to do your fair share however you and she define it. It's the perfect arena to learn compromise.

A rational rather than emotional approach is the best start. Your job is to work together to make the team—and the house—function. Your home is a visible symbol of your life together. Cooperation is what works here, not competition. Work together so that house chores don't get in the way of your happiness with her.

List all the jobs that go under the heading "Housekeeping." Assign yourself those items on the list that you either enjoy or don't mind, and that you can physically accomplish. Ask her to do the same. No scorecards or game playing or power trips here; just do it, and don't count who has the most jobs or who is the biggest breadwinner.

For jobs you both enjoy, like weeding (for the exercise) or walking the dog (for the pleasant neighborhood walk), trade off or share the work. You might also use the opportunity to work together. It's another chance at intimacy.

Apportion the remaining items equitably. If neither of you enjoys mowing the lawn (and you're stronger), you do it. If neither of you wants to grocery shop (and she has more time), she should do it. Horse trade on items you both want to avoid. Suppose neither wants to do laundry. Options include

1. each washes his or her own clothes (not too practical);
2. trade the job back and forth;
3. do it as a joint project (romantically folding sheets together);
4. have someone else do it (if you can afford it or can teach the kids to do it); and
5. let it pile up until one of you gets desperate and does it resentfully. (Watch out for this last one; it's tempting.)

There aren't that many options, and some housekeeping jobs have to get done. (You can't keep wearing dirty socks.) Ask who's more qualified or able. Who would hate it the least? Work together on this project and be honest.

Above all, get housekeeping out of the arena of struggle. Cooperate, don't compete. If it's important to you that one of you absolutely has to wash the windows, and she never gets around to it—do it yourself. Find something positive in it. Think of it as an opportunity to let in the light.

Sometimes the problem is differing standards.

- *It has to be vacuumed how often?*
- *I wonder if I can wear this once more before laundering it?*
- *It looks clean to me. How clean does it have to be?*
- *Why make it? We're only going to get back into it tonight.*
- *The neighbors will think we live in a sty.*
- *I'm not compulsive, I just like things neat and tidy.*

We all have different standards of neat and clean. As a husband, you've got your wife's standards to deal with along with your own. If she's responsible for a particular housekeeping job and you don't like the way she's doing it, tell her. Suggest a realistic, alternative way, but be prepared to do it yourself. (Your standards may be so different from hers, you may be the only one capable of meeting them.) Perhaps you can renegotiate the job for one you now do. Or, of course, you can change your standards. Weigh the cost of the trade-off both to you and to your marriage.

A husband approaches housekeeping with a positive attitude. There's always a way to get it done.

28

Keeping Secrets

Everyone keeps secrets. Or tries to.

Back in the 50s and 60s, Art Linkletter hosted a TV show in which he asked kids about their families. Frequently he got a youngster to say embarrassing things about life at home, like the color of Mom's corset. (Well, at least it seemed embarrassing in those days.) In a similar vein, the 70s and 80s brought us *The Newlyweds,* the game show that rewarded husbands and wives for matching their spouse's secret answers to leading questions (usually leading to the boudoir). People loved those shows. There's nothing like the sense of stealing a peek at someone else's private life.

Your job is to keep your family's private life private.

Whether or not you and your wife keep things secret from each other, you certainly keep things secret from others—from children, from the rest of the family, from your friends. Intimate details of your sex life, your finances, the innermost feelings and thoughts you share together—all these and more are private matters which you choose not to share with anyone else. They become your joint secrets.

Your job is to keep them, even if you become an ex-husband. Let's face it, some of us are ex-husbands. But that's not an excuse for breaking a promise of secrecy. A husband keeps his word, even when it was unspoken. In the noblest sense of the word, a husband is a gentleman.

You may want the world to function in complete candor and honesty, but it doesn't. People keep secrets. Or at least they try. Most of us are not very good at secrecy; we seem to need to tell someone what's going on. So you may have to work hard at this. But do it anyway. Preserve the sanctity of your private married life.

In an odd way, secrets (such as her erotic fantasies or how much you owe on your credit card) can create a closeness that nothing else in your life can. You share this knowledge with each other and no one else. It's a bond.

Of course, you'll want to guard against keeping too many secrets. If you're dogged by the sense of having to keep up a false front to impress those omnipresent "Joneses," it may be time to check your priorities. Keeping secrets takes energy. Reserve it for important concerns. Excessive secretiveness also prevents close friendships from developing. Find a balance.

What about keeping secrets from each other? Except for the obvious—presents, surprise parties, and the like—it's not a good idea. Sometimes a close friend will confide in you and ask you specifically not to tell your wife. Or worse, you'll do something you're ashamed of and would be too chagrined to tell her. Try to head off these situations. Tell friends up front that you don't like keeping things from her. Your friends are important, and if you give your word, don't break it; but get your priorities straight. And if you find yourself doing things you can't tell your wife, it may be time for yet another priorities check. Honesty with your marriage partner has lifelong rewards.

One major exception is details about past loves. By definition, they're past. Any information that goes much beyond surface facts is uncalled for. How would intimate details of a previous romance serve your marriage? If you knew these sorts of details about her, would that knowledge make you a better husband? What would you do with the information?

In pretty much all other areas though, the trust that comes from sharing yourself with her lays a major cornerstone in the structure of your marriage. Without it, whole portions of the building are weakened. Both the person not trusting and the person not trusted feel bad, and rebuilding the foundation takes a lot of time and effort. And what's worse, the stresses on the structure are difficult to locate and identify. You feel uneasy or she feels uneasy, and you don't know why. You tend to disbelieve each other. Not a wise practice for people who intend growing old together.

Remember you're together to help each other grow. And you can't grow if you hide things from her. A good rule of thumb is to check how difficult it is to say something. The harder it is, the more important that you say it. Sometimes the toughest things to say are the ones that help us grow the most.

A husband keeps secrets with his wife, not from her.

29

Keeping the Faith

Everybody believes in something.

Whether you place your highest value in social justice, in a concept of service to God, or in just raising loving children, your values are an integral part of you. Keeping the faith doesn't mean adhering to a specific religious doctrine, although religion plays an important part in many husbands' lives. It means holding to your values and making them a part of your married life.

As you've discovered by now, life usually brings you challenges that test your values, that defy you to keep the faith. Facing such tests together with your wife provides you with useful opportunities—a way to practice your values together, to help each other keep the faith.

You are not on this marriage road by accident. Rule 1 reminds you that you guys didn't find each other because of some fluke. No matter how you personally choose to travel through life's lessons, or at what speed, your mate is your spiritual colleague as well as your physical and emotional travel partner. You're here to help each other. Keep the faith that when you live up to your values and do your best, things will work out for the highest good of all concerned, and thus for your marriage.

Here are some ways to keep the faith:

- **Examine** your beliefs and values. Talk to your wife about them. Ask her about hers, and explore the ways you can travel the road together. If you are religious, for example, perhaps you can study or attend services together.

- **Commit** to live your values. Let this commitment show in your community involvement, in your choice of entertainment, in how expansively you live your life. Remember, too, that your children learn by imitating your behavior; you are being a role model in this all-important area of their education—instilling values.

- **Support** your wife by being there when she needs your help, both in figuring out what she believes and in living it. And step back when she needs to go inside herself. In other words, if you pray together, terrific; but if she needs to meditate alone or go on retreat or volunteer at a literacy program, your job is to bolster her efforts.

- **Understand** that each of your journeys is unique. You may both have strong, abiding, unshakable faith, but this is ultimately an individual voyage. She gets to choose her values for herself—as do you. You guys can disagree and still sustain a loving marriage.

Keeping the faith is easier when husbands and wives share similar beliefs about how the universe works, since our beliefs usually underlie our value systems. Often, a man will be in synch with his wife in this area. You hear a lot of men say, "I married her because we think the same way, and we share the same values."

But even when you and she have identical beliefs, you may occasionally disagree on how to bring them and your values into your life. *What is your position on the proposed new homeless shelter that's supposed to open down the street? What will you tell your son or daughter about birth control? What is our individual responsibility to protect the environment?* And when you disagree (belonging to different religions, for example), the challenge to integrate the values into your life can be truly complicated.

If you have serious differences in beliefs or values, you can at least bring some harmony, if only by following Rule 2, by honoring and respecting your differences. In the end, you are each responsible for your own itinerary through life. Look to your partner for encouragement, support, and understanding, but know that accountability stares at you from the mirror. You can't *make* her believe something, and vice versa.

So don't judge. Travel with her when you can Be there when she needs you. And learn what you can to help you travel your own road.

A husband keeps the faith.

CHAPTER

30

Listening

Men and women listen differently.

As Deborah Tannen points out in her excellent studies of men and women in conversation, there are striking gender differences in how we talk and listen. It's not that one way is right and the other wrong—they're just different. And certainly no one likes to be blamed for these differences, to be told, "You never listen to me."

So what can a husband do? Trying to adopt your wife's style of listening is probably a waste of time and energy; it wouldn't be you, and it wouldn't work. (Just as it would be fruitless for her to try to change her style to yours, even though you wish she would.)

As with everything else in this manual (and in your marriage), you are aiming for the ideal. In this case, the ideal is a husband who actively listens to his wife. Here's what he does:

1. He listens willingly because he's interested in her. Perhaps not in everything she says or in how she says it, but in her as a person. He gives her his full attention.
2. He tries to see things as she sees them. Not to agree with (or even to enjoy) what she's saying, but to understand her and her *come-from*.
3. He senses her underlying feelings and pays attention to her non-verbal communication. Often her body language and tone communicate more than her words.
4. He hears her out—a good precedent for when he wants her to listen to him without interruption or prejudgment. This means no scowling, head shaking, or sarcasm.

77

5. Particularly when he can tell she's irritated, he repeats back to her (in an even, noncritical tone) what she has said, so she'll know he heard her. This simple technique usually has an astonishingly calming effect.

Sounds like a tall order, but what's the alternative? Living out the sitcom version of the man who never listens to his long-suffering wife? What a drag.

Listening doesn't mean agreeing or obeying; it means following the simple guidelines described above. Understand what you are doing: you are bridging the gap between the way you and your wife understand each other. You may have to invest in a few new behaviors (looking at her while listening, for example), but you'll appreciate the return on the investment in your marriage.

In addition, good listeners are better liked than bad listeners. If you listen well, your wife will like it, and it will serve your marriage. Besides, if you want her to listen to you, listen to her.

A husband is a good listener.

31

Loving Only Her

Everyone always tells us to love one another. When it comes to sex, however, everyone other than your wife is best loved from a distance.

People have been testing theories of affairs and extra-marital relationships for quite some time now. The consensus is they're not good for your marriage. Forget all the "negative" reasons for remaining faithful; they've been preached ad nauseam: *It's morally sinful; It's ethically wrong since you pledged your truth; it won't look good at your confirmation hearing, etc.* But instead of resigning yourself to monogamy because the alternative is unpleasant, focus on the positive side. A husband who observes his vow of fidelity honors his wife and serves his marriage. He also keeps his word.

A husband is faithful, loyal, and true. Besides, he knows that monogamy has a lot going for it:

- It allows you to trust and be trusted.
- It's safe.
- It expresses love and allows you to do something with each other that you do with no one else—a unique bonding.

So what do you do with those "wild oats" you haven't sown? What about the hunt, the pursuit, the conquest? What do you do with those seemingly uncontrollable urges? All that energy has to go someplace, biologists and psychologists tell us. And there's a ring of truth to what they say. So where to put it?

With your wife. You are the one who determines where your energies go—all of them. When it comes to your attraction to a woman, your most important body parts are your heart and your mind.

If you sense an attraction to someone other than your wife, step back from it for a moment. Observe yourself. *What's missing in my life with my wife that I*

have this hormonal attraction? It may be something obvious—some ignored problem that has festered. Or perhaps the subtlest of holding back by one or both of
you.

Probably it's not just the surface stuff, even though folks usually blame minor things. Whether she's gotten out of shape or you've spent time together
"too much" lately or you've been together "too long"—all these can be over-
come when we don't hold onto them as smoke screens. Chances are, something else requires your attention, and you would do well to pay it heed. A
choice to serve your long-term marriage interests is always the wisest.

The sexual part of your male energy belongs with her.

You can make your wife the object of your sexuality—all of it. Focus your
energy on her body, her sensuality; lavish your affection on her. Create an image in your mind of the perfect love partner for you at this moment: she's it.
You feel lusty at her sensual beauty. She's what fills all your fantasies, your
dream girl, the object of all your sexual energy. You choose to be excited by her.
If something is holding you back and getting in the way, be willing to let it go
gently.

How can you control such things? The fact is, you do it all the time. Remem-
ber a time when you felt sad about something—a lost job, perhaps even a death?
At one point you decided to cheer up, to get past the sadness with an effort of
will. You moved from one state of feeling to another. You shifted your feelings.
Or perhaps you held a grudge against someone until you chose to forgive him.
Remember how your feelings changed to relief as soon as you made that choice?
You've frequently been able to put aside hurt feelings when you wanted to.

It can work with love feelings, too. If you *choose* to make her the object of
your passion, and you do the work to get through anything that gets in the way,
you can achieve it. It's a conscious choice that will serve your marriage. Find a
way.

A husband loves his wife only.

32

Making Love

This is the sex chapter, and it starts with two truths that many people either deny or are unaware of:

1. Everyone's sex drive is different.
2. Each of us is responsible for his or her own sexual pleasure.

Is there a subject more written about than sex? (Well, maybe God and raising children, but it's close.) Let's keep it simple, because this is a complex subject. Here are your instructions:

Own Your Sexuality
Communicate
Exult

Owning your sexuality may not be as easy as it sounds.

Whatever your attitudes toward sex are, they're yours. Some come from your parents, some from your religious tradition. Others come from your sexual experiences with others, from your exposure to magazine articles or movies or TV, and from sharing opinions and stories with other men. It doesn't matter where they come from; they belong to you now. Own them. Acknowledge what your feelings are—even those you'd like to change (for example, those that stem from a poor self-image due to being physically out of shape).

Your wife has her version.

You have chosen her as your sole sex partner, and she has done the same. Now your attitudes toward sex are blended. They belong to you, plural. It's your job to smooth this ongoing merger, no matter how different the two inputs may be.

A husband knows that his sexual drives, needs, and desires are not always the same as his wife's. He also knows what she expects of him—or thinks he knows.

A husband may sometimes be cranky because he isn't "getting enough." He may sometimes be uneasy because he feels he has to perform whenever she's in the mood. And sometimes he's anxious or worried because (take your pick) he can't perform at the same peaks as before, he fears being compared to previous lovers, his wife does not respond to his touch when he wants her to, he doesn't feel as attracted to her as he used to, or he's got some hang-ups he'd prefer not to deal with "just yet."

If you or your wife has attitudes about sex which you have trouble dealing with (almost everyone does), do something about it. Don't blame her if your sex life isn't all you want it to be. And don't blame yourself. Blaming only serves to make somebody wrong. It's easy to blame her or to blame life for "mismatching" you. It's much harder, and ultimately more rewarding, to take responsibility for your part in how you feel and what you can do about it.

• • •

The best way to start dealing is to acknowledge what you feel and what you expect. Communicate. Discussions of sex needn't be limited to locker rooms and powder rooms.

Rule 2 reminds us to let go of expectations. Your sexuality is the best place to start. Let's face it, you've got some sexual expectations of your wife. You expect her to feel, think, and act in certain ways. You expect her to be in synch with your needs and desires. She probably has similar expectations.

One way to let go of expectations is to communicate them.

Problems with trust arise when you feel judged on how well you perform (if only by your own standards). They often center on frequency of intercourse, quality of erection, or degree of pleasure you produce in your wife.

Trust her with this intimate information. Acknowledge how you judge yourself, ask for her input on the subject, and trust what she says. You'll know if she's being honest. A difficult task? Perhaps, but if you've got some problem areas, they're not going to go away by ignoring them.

Do you want to please her? Then ask her how and trust it. If it requires changing some past behaviors, do it. Don't assume that what "worked" with a previous partner will please her. She's the best judge of what she prefers.

Do you want her to please you? Tell her how. Don't blame her for not knowing if you've never told her. Talk about your love making and about what you like doing and what brings you pleasure. Sexual trust building through communication will serve your marriage well.

• • •

Exult and be jubilant in your sex life.

Both of you have changed somewhat since you first felt sexual stirrings for each other. If you're lucky, you've moved toward each other, and your sex life has become safe and exciting. What a combination!

If the thrill is less than it was during courtship, don't let others set standards for you. Set your own standards of love making. Frequency, intensity, playfulness—no one can tell you how to balance these except you and her. The only rules are the rules *you* set.

Who initiates? When is a good time? What to do about birth control? Can we experiment with different activities? These and dozens of other questions can be answered by only you and your wife. The more of these you answer together, the better your sex life becomes. The better your sex life becomes, the more you get to exult in this pleasure. And what better way to celebrate life!

A husband is a true lover.

33

Making Love Last

How do they do it? Those few couples you've known in your life who seem to have strong, loving relationships that endure for decades. How do they make love last? Were they just lucky in finding the "perfect" partner? Probably not, though if you asked them, that might be what they'd say, because each has become the perfect partner—or as good a one as possible.

Making love last is about an abiding confidence in your marriage and its staying power: Keeping your vision alive.

Let's face it, living with someone is not simple. In fact, living with a person you're going to grow old with can be complex and arduous. The daily stuff of life gets in the way; your needs conflict with hers; you occasionally irritate each other. You begin to lose sight of your vision.

The good news is, it's not a terminal condition.

With any luck, you've got a healthy, intense, enthusiastic desire for your wife, and your sex life enhances your love. Along with all the other good parts in your marriage, you want this to last, too. You can make it so.

Steps for making love last:
1. **Celebrate your marriage**. Take her out as though you were still dating. Buy her a present impulsively. Be romantic regularly, allowing a courtly side to your relationship. Even if you're not a romantic kind of guy, sometimes leading her to the dance floor has a way of bringing rhythm to your feet. And get organized about remembering her birthday and other events she enjoys celebrating. Find fun, creative ways to love her actively. Tell her how much you love your life together. She'll love it and it will keep love alive. What you're doing here is taking the lead in the Dance of Life.

85

2. **Define and refine your vision**. (See the "Goals" part of Chapter 1.) You both need to be conscious of the vital part your joint vision plays in your life together. Think about it and talk about it as it deepens and changes and grows. What do you stand for together? It will help you recommit to your marriage periodically. Your anniversary is a good time. Make it private—just the two of you, face to face. Talk about where you are and where you'd like to be. Let her know what's going on with you. If you don't like some things about yourself or the marriage, tell her. Tell the good stuff, too—the parts you appreciate. Also tell her what you'd like to see change. Make known your promises and intentions to her and to the marriage (kind of like renewing your wedding vows, only updating them).

3. **Own your power**. Not physical power, but the inner power to continually reconfigure your life. Let go of past personal hurts that still plague you. If you stubbornly hold onto things that get in the way of your marriage, let them go. You are a unique life on this planet and you have all you need to shape that life. Know your inner strength and use it.

A husband is an active, dynamic participant in his marriage. He enthusiastically joins in the dance. He makes love last by keeping love alive.

CHAPTER

34

Negotiating

Wally is seated comfortably on the living room sofa reading the paper when the phone rings. Marsha, within his line of sight, is taking her turn doing the dishes. Wally looks up as if to say, "Oh, could that be the phone?" and slowly begins to put down the paper. Marsha says, "Don't bother, I'll get it."

We have just witnessed a full-fledged negotiation.

Husbands and wives negotiate all the time. And not just about the more obvious stuff of life—where to live, what color to paint the walls, how much money gets spent on clothing. Smaller negotiations go on continually—blanket sharing in the middle of the night, who gets up to comfort the baby, who says "I'm sorry" first. Few couples get through a day without negotiating in one form or another.

Recognize the fact that you don't always negotiate fairly. Sometimes you don't even realize you're negotiating. It's a large part of your communication, and it's best to face up to what's going on. The more you negotiate openly, the better your life will be and the fewer hidden resentments will build up to sabotage you.

Your job is to negotiate fairly. Hold up your end ethically and seek always to serve your marriage. If you find yourselves bickering or arguing or fighting about issues, try negotiating instead. (See the chapter on Fighting.)

The negotiating goal is to reconcile differences, with your integrity intact. In other words, to figure out how you both can "win" without compromising your personal ethics or morality. And you can do it. Negotiating is an integral part of marital communications. Here's how:

1. **Deal with your differences**. Acknowledge your problems, and bring them up when you both have the time and energy to deal with them positively. Suffering in sullen silence doesn't serve either of you.

2. **Stand on the same side of the table**. The past two decades have produced a sea of excellent books on negotiating, followed closely by waves of negotiation consultants called in to train government and business leaders. One of their major insights: Negotiation works best when one genuinely recognizes the needs of the other as legitimate. In their version of this truth, Hugh and Gayle Prather draw a lovely metaphor in *A Book for Couples*. They suggest that instead of seeing your wife as an opponent, put the matter on the table and stand next to her (not across from her). Now the two of you are both working to solve it; you are looking at it together, both on the same side of the table. *What can we do to make this right?*

3. **Commit to finding a solution**. Be willing to be flexible, to compromise, and to follow through. If you're not, you'll end up bullying or being bullied. Brainstorming helps. Look for alternatives; avoid assuming there's only one answer. If you want your brother to come over for dinner once a week and she doesn't, perhaps you can occasionally go with him on a "boys' night out" for pizza. Note how you view things differently and then look for common interests. It works for world leaders seeking peace, why not you? You've got your love in common as a starter.

4. **Don't make her "wrong."** That makes you "right," so you'll want her to lose (because she's *wrong*). You only want winners in this marriage. Attacking problems is better than attacking people. Being tough on the dilemma (not her) prevents bruised egos.
   You're a good cook; it's just that I like less salt in my food, so I want to add it myself.

5. **Guilt peddling is out**. For both of you. Don't be susceptible if she tries to make you feel bad about the past. You did the best you could at the time. Stay in the present.

6. **Changing your mind is okay**. So is being unpredictable. It makes a lot more sense to admit a change of heart than to waste energy proving to yourself or her that you haven't had one.
   Any time she refuses to negotiate, ask why. Then negotiate that. Show how it will benefit her to negotiate. Figure out her needs and describe how they can be met by talking about them. Perhaps offer concessions first.

The bottom line: Prepare and be fair. Husbands negotiate fairly.

35

Opening Doors
and stuff like that

Surely the smallest Boy Scout has learned that it doesn't count as a good deed to help an old lady across the street if she doesn't want to cross the street. Or if she doesn't want to be helped.

Miss Manners

Opening a door for someone is courteous and practical. It shows respect and elevates the moment with a touch of grace. What could be wrong with that?

Showing politeness and graciousness is a practical way of getting along with people. They like you better. They're less likely to put up barriers between you because you've lowered your own barriers by an act of consideration.

It doesn't matter that the word *gentleman* was defined by the actions of courtesans or chivalrous knights of long ago. It might just as easily have developed that *lady* meant all those attitudes and behaviors—politeness, attentiveness, a readiness to help. It doesn't matter.

What matters is that being a gentleman works whether your lady fair is a full time homemaker, a carpenter, or an attorney for the prosecution. It's ennobling; it makes you a better person.

In the early days of modern feminism, many said that such classic gentlemanliness implied power, and worse, a debt or weakness by the woman. If such courtesies imply this to you or your mate, by all means avoid them. But if you can accept such gestures as one sublime area in which there is no return expected, do it. And do it naturally—not because it's some big deal. There's a nobility in that warrior deep inside you, and gentlemanliness is part of its best expression.

So, be a gentleman full-heartedly with your wife. She deserves the best of your respect and graciousness. And demonstrating those qualities is one of the main jobs of being a husband.

What if she objects? To some such behaviors, she probably will. Taken to an extreme, gentlemanliness could get silly. The goal here is not to become a servant, it's to serve your marriage. You don't have to open every door, uncap every pickle jar, carry every package, pay the check at every restaurant to practice being a gentleman. Work it out with her. Notice which behaviors she appreciates. Which jobs would she rather do for herself?

Decide for yourselves what comprises this behavior in your marriage. If between the two of you, you decide that it's her job to register you in at hotels, then offering to do it for her would be counterproductive. That's not to say you wouldn't help out once in a while. There are no losers here, only winners. A husband behaves in a gentlemanly way because it serves his marriage, his wife, and him.

Should you hold open a door for her? Should you offer to bring her a cup of tea when she's tired? Should you refill her wine glass at dinner? Of course you should. You are not implying that she cannot perform these actions for herself, you are gallantly showing respect.

Naturally, you can't expect your wife to adjust to every conduct that you consider gentlemanly. Treat her the way she wants to be treated. Ask her to do the same for you. Adding a level of loving dignity to your marriage will serve it well.

A husband is a gentleman.

36

Posturing

posturing: *assuming an attitude merely for effect.*

Macho man is alive and kicking! Aggressive, virile, and domineering behaviors are still admired and glorified in much of our world. And to some extent, we're comfortable with the role. Part of us wants to be that way. And when we don't feel it, to at least look the part. So we posture.

As with much of life, the trick is finding the right balance. How much of our manliness is based on inner strength and how much on looking the part?

Sometimes posturing works on our jobs. A salesman offers an enthusiastic hand even if he's in the dumps; a repairman speaks confidently even if he doesn't have a clue what the problem is; a policeman talks tough to a thief even if he's scared.

But posturing almost never works at home. Some husbands put on a brave front before their wives even though in pain or grieving; some assume a know-it-all act even when uncertain; some exaggerate sexual potency even when....

Share yourself with her. Let her know what you feel and think. Honesty is good for your marriage. The less posturing you do, the better. (See the chapter "Expressing Your Feelings.")

What if you have a headache but don't want to make a big deal about it or worry her? You take aspirin and it goes away. No harm. The harm comes when you repeatedly posture over bigger things. You know what they are. Don't do it. More often than not, a macho posture hides you. And a husband needs to be seen.

A husband is a visible, genuine person.

37

Raising Children

This is not a father's manual, but the essence of what makes a good husband also makes a good father. Successful husbands know that what benefits them most is humor and lightness, passion and joy for life, and trust. Fathers need these qualities, and more.

Whatever your code of personal ethics may be, live it. Your kids will know. It's time to stop giving any validity to "Do as I say, not as I do." No one has ever obeyed that order, and no one ever will. We learn by watching, by example.

We learned our most important skills by imitation. We didn't read or think about walking or speaking or eating. We imitated. We learned by example.

We also learned to face our fears, by example. We also developed an image of what a father does, by example. Your children will learn from you, by example. You want your kids to imitate the best parts of you, so be the best part of you. Their image of what a father does comes from you.

• • •

Parenting is no small task. Over the years you and your wife will have many disagreements over "what's best for the children." You two can have legitimate differences of opinion, but guard against your ego taking over. It's not important who thought of an idea or who was right or whom a child looks to for nurturing. What's important is what's best for them, and that they see you working together as a team to figure that out. Not only are power struggles usually counterproductive, but they also teach your kids how husbands and wives deal with differences, by example.

One of the classic mother-father disagreements is about discipline. It seems to be a rule that in every two-parent family, one is strict with the kids and one is lenient—a balancing act that also goes on inside most of us. We try to stay balanced between the two extremes. *Do I trust completely or do I hold back? Do I come more from love or from fear? Whichever side you're closer to, don't let the difference become so important that it obstructs the continued smooth flow of your marriage.*

Don't let being a good father get in the way of being a good husband. They're not contradictory.

• • •

One of life's most difficult lessons is unqualified love—how to give it; how to accept it. Children provide us with a perfect model for this lesson. They are born loving unconditionally. Learn from them. Learn to give and receive unconditional love. An added bonus: it will serve your marriage.

A husband and father loves unconditionally. He sets a good example.

38

Repairing and Maintaining the Home

Whose job is it to fix the toilet? Who changes light bulbs, splices wires, sees to it that the VCR works? Most couples find that it works best when the husband takes these responsibilities. If you don't have any problems with that role, you can skip this chapter.

Compared to housekeeping, repairing and maintaining seems to put the burden more on you. Is that okay with you? Sure, it's the traditional role of a husband and we're in an age where tradition is questioned, not blindly perpetuated. And sure, you can make a case for mutual responsibility in all things related to sustaining the home. Indeed, if she's handier than you, she should rewire the lamp or snake the kitchen drain. So, why is it assumed to be the husband's job? Because, generally, it works.

You may both have co-equal responsibility for your life together, but one of you has to shoulder the primary duty of repair and maintenance. It is nowhere chiseled in stone that a husband must perform all these tasks, and every family has some differences. In fact, whoever is better at a skill and who wants to perform it, should be allowed to do so. But generally, R&M is your responsibility. Don't make this into a test of feminist principles or of gender equality; it's just your job. It's "husband duty." (So what's a "wife's duty"? Don't worry. You guys will figure that out.)

Being responsible means seeing what needs to be done (perhaps after your mate has pointed it out), ensuring that it gets done, and following up to see that it stays done.

Since this responsibility affects the quality of your life, make sure you are clear and overt about who has it; i.e., make sure you both know whose job it is to change the vacuum cleaner belt or fix the faucet. Or to call an expert in to do it.

95

Enver has a busy day lined up, so he asks Sue to call the plumber, be there to oversee the repairs, and test the end result. She's home today, has the time, and agrees to do it. Even though she will do all the "work," they both acknowledge that getting it done is his responsibility.

Suppose neither of you is handy, and neither wants any part of R&M. Learn. Do it anyway. Or at least learn whom to call and how to deal with plumbers, carpenters, auto mechanics, etc. Shouldering the job of keeping your home functional is vital to its energy. You are creating a secure atmosphere for you and your wife, memories for your children, and a home with its share of your wonderful male energy—the kind of energy that is creative, protective, and warm.

Remember, too, that cheerfulness is important when it comes to setting the boundaries of what you will and won't do. If your wife is pickier than you about "that paint chipping off the porch," you have to decide how far your responsibilities go. How much should you honor her whims? It's up to you. But don't set yourself up for resentment by *I'll-get-around-to-it* false expectations. Let her know how and why you've decided, and when you're available for husband duty.

I know you want the kitchen painted, but I have other priorities this week (like the loose towel rack, the ripped screen, and the new novel I'm reading). I only have so many hours a week for these projects and only so much energy. If it's important enough, perhaps we can do it together or we can hire someone to do it. Otherwise, I'm putting it on my schedule for next month.

A husband is a responsible man.

39

Resisting

Carl's wife asked him to go shopping with her on Saturday afternoon. Carl doesn't much enjoy shopping, although he occasionally accompanies her. On this day however, there was a game on TV he wanted to watch. He calmly said, "I'll pass."

The next day, when Carl's wife asked him to go with her to a concert, he said, "You know I hate classical music." He argued strongly that he should be allowed to do whatever he wants. He ranted and raved about it. How dare she demand that he give up his free time?

The energy Carl expended resisting his wife's suggestion on Sunday was out of proportion to his wife's request—a sure sign that something else was going on for him. If it were a simple matter of not enjoying a certain kind of music, he wouldn't be carrying on like that. If it were simple, he'd have treated it the way he did the shopping request the day before.

Maybe he feels insecure that his wife is better educated than he. Maybe he feels intimidated by his belief that concert goers would look down on the way he dresses. Maybe he's still mad that he was forced to take tuba lessons as a child when he wanted to take art classes instead. Or maybe none of this. But whatever it is, her request has touched a raw nerve. Carl can use that sensation of resistance as a compass to point him toward a lesson.

Rule 1 tells us to use everything for our learning. Does that mean that Carl (or you) should force himself to go to concerts? Absolutely not. But it may mean doing something to improve his self-esteem (or his wardrobe), if that's the problem. Outbursts are signals that something needs realignment. Whenever you find yourself resisting something strenuously, check your energy level. The more energy you feel, the more likely there's something for you to learn. Whatever you resist persists. So move toward its lesson instead.

A husband weighs and considers the truth in the saying, *Sometimes that which is best for me is that into which I go kicking and screaming the loudest.*

40

Saying No

Pierre could never say no to his wife. He wanted to, but always found a good excuse for saying yes: he didn't want a hassle; he was too tired to argue; he felt insecure in their relationship and wanted to please her; he never learned how to negotiate or to speak up for himself; or perhaps he just didn't know why.

Over time he came to resent her: She was too demanding of him. He felt powerless: She was to blame as the "cause" of his bad feelings. Why didn't she see that he was too busy or tired to go to the store right now?

The resentments festered and his marriage suffered.

The danger of becoming Pierre is real for some men. Eventually, resentments subtly but persistently erode the closeness in a marriage. They chafe and alienate affections, and that's bad news for a relationship.

Most books on saying no have been written for women, but men have the problem, too. Sometimes it's hard to say no, especially to your wife. It's difficult to imagine a day in which a man doesn't wish he'd said no to one or more requests (demands) on his time and energy. The good news: It's a learnable skill.

Commit to learning how to say no—appropriately, assertively, and without guilt. It'll serve your marriage by cutting down on wear and tear. You can even do it diplomatically. Here are some guidelines:

1. **Understand that it's a basic right**. Everyone has the right to exercise free will and say no, particularly when the alternative is to feel taken advantage of. Some people feel guilty about saying no, but that's usually a waste of time. And you can choose not to feel guilt.

   Kay asked Peter to give up his four-times-a-week workouts at the gym so

99

they could spend more time together. He responded: "I want us to have more time together, too, but I'm not willing to cut into the time I spend maintaining fitness. Let's come up with some other way."

Even though this scene may end up with a negotiated compromise (working out together, for example), Peter knew instinctively that he had the right to say no to the specific request. And he did it without rancor.

2. **Be timely and firm**. When you decide to say no, say it as soon as possible and don't sound as though you're hesitating.

   After Jasmine asked him to stop wearing his ratty clothes around the house on Saturdays, Ali considered her request and said: "I know you want to keep a certain image around here, but this is the one day I get to completely kick back. I feel better hanging out in my jeans."

3. **Leave emotion out of it**. Your decision to say no may be based on more than just logic, but communicate it reasonably, perhaps offering suggestions of other ways the request might be met. Explain honestly and briefly without defensiveness or apology.

   I know you want me to be less of a tightwad, as you put it, but I don't think I should. One of us has to be cautious in how we manage our budget, and it feels right for me to play that part in our marriage. We can always compromise, but basically I'm okay being the economical one of the family.

4. **Practice**. It may not make perfect, but it will make better. And remember that whenever anyone (including you) asks someone else (like your wife) to do something, one of the two possible responses is no.

● ● ●

Another kind of saying no is "rejecting the verdict." Rule 2 urges you not to judge or label your wife, but what if she is judgmental toward you? What do you do? In the movie *The Electric Horseman*, Jane Fonda accuses Robert Redford of having a mean streak in him. He looks up thoughtfully, reflects on the observation, and says, "No. No I don't." She judged him, and he rejected the verdict. You can do the same.

You're so mean and inconsiderate. You knew I had a meeting to go to tonight. Why didn't you check with me first? I hate your thoughtlessness.

When your wife addresses a specific behavior (not checking with her, for example), you can either agree or disagree with facts. When she tells of her emotion (hate), you get to hear what she's feeling. Despite the tension that may be in the air in this conversation, you have these two good areas to deal with. But she is also judging you by using some loaded value words (mean, inconsiderate, thoughtless). Judgments like these will not serve your marriage. And you do not have to accept them. Are you, in fact, deliberately unkind to her? If so, that's an area to work on. Mostly, however, you'll be able to say no, you aren't a bad person. And you can refuse the verdict the way Robert Redford did.

No, I am not a mean person. I didn't accept that invitation to hurt you. I know I should have checked; I just forgot. I'll do better. But don't judge me as "mean"; I'm not.

Remind her that people's standards differ, and no one gets to be the standard bearer—the "right" one. Judgments on your worth as a human being will not serve your marriage; you would do well to say no to them.

A husband knows how and when to say no.

41

Sharing Interests

Interest: a pursuit; a feeling of curiosity, concern, or involvement

Paco: *We've tried this before and it doesn't work. You know I don't enjoy going to Save-the-Rain-Forest type meetings.*

Rosa: *I just want us to have some interests in common. You're so busy with work, we don't seem to do much together.*

Paco: *I agree, but we always end up mad at each other after one of these meetings. Why do it? Why don't you come running with me in the mornings if you want a shared interest?*

Rosa: *I could never get up that early.*

You want your marriage to be more than just meals and bed. You sleep, you work, you have hobbies and other friends. As an active man, you need to balance all this plus keep love alive in your marriage. One proven technique for holding up your end in this quest is to spend some quality shared-interest time with your wife.

If Paco does see some benefits to sharing interests with Rosa, here are some of his options:

- Bolster Rosa's interest and stance by being a supportive husband; without participating himself, he can show interest in her pursuits. He can encourage her.

- "Go along for the ride" with an interest of hers. Go with her to the environmental meeting and not make a big deal out of it. In other words, adopt an interest of hers because she wants him to. At least this gives them some time together and something to talk about, even if they disagree.

103

- Better still, find a cause that interests him and try to nudge her in that direction. Perhaps an entirely different interest like local politics or volunteering at a homeless shelter.
- Negotiate. Trade a meeting for a run. The end result has value to him and his marriage.

Sharing interests is more than just having a cookout with the neighbors once a week. It's going dancing, enjoying sports, playing bridge, attending the theater, discussing movies, the news, or metaphysics—all kinds of stuff that can add to your individual and joint experience of life. Husbands who have at least some common interests with their wives have more interesting marriages.

Another type of shared interest is in her career. Listen to her work-related concerns, anecdotes, and ambitions. Her job, even if it's homemaking, is her interest. Pay attention to her aspirations and worries. When she complains, be compassionate; she's asking for consideration of what's important to her. Being a good role model in this regard is the best way to encourage similar behavior from her.

Perhaps Paco also needs to decide the importance of developing interests outside of work. Maybe he needs a separate pursuit for his own personal growth. Hobbies and avocations don't have to be shared with a spouse to have value. In fact, all husbands need separate identities and some separate interests to continue to be interesting spouses.

A husband shares some common interests with his wife. He knows that to be interesting, he has to be interested.

42

Sharing the Wealth

Linda: *I hate to ask this, but I was wondering if you guys could put me up for a week 'til my first paycheck comes and I can get a place of my own.*

Janet: *Gee, if it were up to me, I'd really like to help you out, but you know Sam likes his privacy. I'm afraid....*

Linda: *Oh, you don't have to explain. Um....I understand. I'll just work something out....*

Chances are one of you feels more generous than the other, is more inclined to give to the needy, sees the world as an abundant universe. The other is more concerned about preserving what you have, making sure any causes or people you help are deserving, and not getting scammed. Whichever one you are, your marriage affords you a chance to re-examine the roles that charity and service play in your lives.

A husband is in service to his wife and his family first. Charity, after all, does begin at home. And by now you know that charity means more than just giving a few bucks or some old clothes to a worthy cause. It means opening your heart, listening to and comforting people, and spending time and energy in giving. And that part definitely starts at home. You may not instantly be able to change the world, but you can have an immediate effect on your smaller world—your family.

When it comes to the outside world, two generous spouses have a marvelous magnifying effect on each other. However, when one is a grouch....er, rather, a cautious person (watch those labels!), that spouse can have a dampening effect on the do-gooder mate.

If you are the partner with more compassion, the following guidelines should be easy. If not, think about what they mean to you. Find ways to apply them in your life. Make them integral parts of your vision for your life together.

105

1. **Do what you can for people**. Ask yourself a question: *How much time do I spend trying to get out of doing for others?* If you're even slightly chagrinned by the answer, do something about it. To encourage selfless-ness in the world, practice it yourself. If your wife is involved in service activities, follow her lead and join her where possible. Set standards for yourself and live up to them. (Hint: Telling your wife about these stan-dards makes them more real and motivates you more to act in accor-dance with them.)

2. **Pace yourself**. A husband combines work, play, and contribution to his world. All are important. Each has it's place in his life. Too much of one, and not enough of the other two, causes imbalance. Most of us have a tendency to spend too much time in the work corner of this triangle. Then we get overloaded and go to the play corner (vacation). Don't ig-nore the service corner. Its dividends will spill over into other areas of your life.

3. **Know your possibilities**. True, you're only one person, but you *can* make a difference. You already do. Just by your existence and presence, you influence those in your life, most particularly your wife.

4. **Assume an abundant universe**. We all know stories about the poorest family on the block who, nonetheless, are the first ones to help others in times of trouble. Giving makes you feel as though you have more than enough, and that feeling has a way of perpetuating itself. Compassion and redemption go hand in hand.

A husband values and shares his family's bounty.

43

Socializing

Yes, it does seem to be an unwritten rule: Almost every marriage comes with one party animal and one couch potato.

Some people gain energy by being around other people. Their spouses typically don't. In other words, one person feels more alive around people, while another feels stronger and more refreshed through time spent alone. Is one of these ways right and the other wrong? Of course not.

When you and your wife are both the same type, no problems. Either you'd both rather stay home to read or watch TV or perhaps go out alone to dinner and a movie. OR you both enjoy having others around frequently. Perhaps your home is a natural gathering place for your friends. Either way, revel in your good fortune. Openly acknowledge how much you enjoy having a mate who shares this energy.

But what if you're opposites? What if you're more inclined to turn down party invitations while she looks forward to them? What if, on the other hand, you love going out and "working" a crowd of new people, while she likes the idea of cuddling on the sofa and falling asleep by 10 p.m.?

This is another one of those perfect opportunities for compromise: Friday nights the two of you alone, and Saturday nights the world—or some such arrangement. Compromise can take many forms, but beware of setting up a balance sheet. No one likes to hear, "We've been to three parties this month, and I've only gotten one night home alone with you."

Instead of looking at the tradeoffs as something you give up, try looking at it as a chance for you to try out new behaviors. If you're going to live with her the rest of your life, you'll have to learn to adapt.

"That's just who I am," you say. "I've always been that way. Besides, my personality is perfect for my job." In other words, Why would you want to change anything? Two reasons:

1. If you take Rule 1 to heart, it's not an accident that you found her. You have something to learn from her. (And she has something to learn from you.) This may be part of it.
2. Balance is the order of nature. When your life is in balance, you're in harmony with your life. If you are one extreme and she's the other, you both may be served by more balance.

If you are the more socially introverted partner, ask yourself: *What is there about being more outgoing that might be good for me and my marriage? Was I attracted to her because she had these outgoing qualities (not in spite of them)? Might I have something to learn here?* Natural born hermits will never learn to love big parties, nor should they. But making a little effort is likely to open up some new possibilities for you.

The same holds true of the opposite situation. Suppose you're the extrovert, the one who always wants to be on the go, to be where there's action, to mix it up. *What is there about looking inward that might serve me and my marriage? What value do I see in adopting some of her quieter nature?*

You can't *make* her different; you're the only one you can change. But perhaps you can make it easier for her to see your side. If something is important to you, tell her.

It would mean a lot to me to have you enjoy the games with me. I'd really appreciate it.

Identifying yourself as extrovert or introvert can be misleading. Few people are invariably one extreme or the other, so don't lock yourself in with a label. Labels sometimes make us subtly feel we have to live up to them. And you certainly don't want to give up your pleasures. Go out and watch the game with your own friends; attend the gallery opening with other art lovers; bowl or play bridge with people who share the same passion. Or stay home and read a book while she goes out. You don't have to do everything together. The idea is to learn from your differences, not to give up who you are.

A husband finds a balance.

44

Solving Her Problems

Her: *Everything went wrong today! I forgot some papers and had to come back home after getting half-way to work; then I got stuck in traffic. The Interstate is always backed up!*

You: *Well, in the future, take the back roads. Here, I'll show you on the map.*

Her: *Then my boss decided to table my proposal—the one I've been working on for 3 weeks. I was furious!*

You: *You probably didn't include the kind of cost benefits the company wanted to see. I could help you work up some new figures. We'll use my new spreadsheet software.*

Her: *Will you stop trying to solve my problems!*

You: *I'm only trying to help. Why take it out on me?*

Why? Well, first because you're closest. But primarily, because you are a problem solver, and she doesn't want her problems solved. At least, not right now she doesn't. You see a puzzle and immediately set to seeking a solution. If something doesn't work, you fix it—right away. Trouble is, right now she doesn't want anything fixed. She wants to complain a little; she wants some sympathy and understanding; she wants time to recover. It doesn't matter that your suggestions may ultimately help her. What she wants is a safe place to vent some frustrations.

And sometimes the exact opposite may be true. Occasionally, she will feel so thwarted by life she will want you to take over for a while and be the competent, complete problem solver.

So, how are you to know what to do?

You could ask. (Of course, asking an upset person, "How can I help?" could easily be, to put it mildly, unproductive.) Better still, you could crank up your husband's intuition antenna.

When your wife has a problem, it's your job to be there for her. If she wants you to be her hero and come to the rescue, put on your finest knight's suit and solve her problems the best you can. But it's the poorly timed pushing of solutions that generates resentment. Be sensitive to her situational needs. You may want to help her solve the problems, but your primary job is to gently help her move through her frustration. Offering help is only one of the ways.

Some people have trouble accepting help under any circumstances, most especially when they haven't asked for it. If you and your wife play out this scene from time to time, notice how it never goes anywhere. In this situation, you have different needs; hers is for sympathy and yours is to be helpful. You both want something but neither gets it. You guys are bright enough to try an approach that meets both your needs.

Here's how:
Before you go into an automatic problem solver mode, do three things:

1. **Check her needs level**. Is she low on hugs? She may need one. Perhaps a long, quiet cuddle. Maybe she needs some alone time or some time to holler without getting any feedback at all. Take the kids for a walk. Listen. What are her immediate needs?

2. **Use your head**. You know from past experience that she is not receptive to solutions when she's angry or frustrated. How long does it usually take for her to calm down? Wait until the time is right. Good problem solvers know the importance of good timing. The goal is to solve problems, not cause more frustration.

3. **When you offer help, don't thrust it**. Be kindly as you offer your input, your insights, your expertise. And don't take offense if she rejects it. She's not rejecting you; she may want to sort things out on her own. It's often the best way to learn. People are most receptive to aid when it's not forced on them and when they are not made to feel incompetent. Reminding her that she's got what it takes to solve problems on her own may be the best help you can give.

When the roles are reversed (when you need her empathy and tenderness), let her know. If she's a natural problem solver, take advantage of her insights, but tell her what your present needs are. Explain what's going on with you. Problem solvers can't always guess what's going on in another's mind; they're too preoccupied with the challenge of setting things right.

This kind of situation, while irritating, needn't overwhelm you because you both are capable of understanding what's needed to get past it.

A husband "gets it" about solving problems.

45

Spending and Saving Money

- *What's the point in having money if we can't enjoy it now? We're success-ful, and I want to show it in how I dress, how you dress, what we drive, where we live—the whole nine yards. Get it back on the market as fast as possible, I always say.*
- *You and that outward show! I can take it or leave it. For me, money repre-sents security for our old age. I'd rather save and make sure we don't end up old and poor. We can't go overboard.*

The chapter on Breadwinning discusses how money is provided, the one on Bill Paying and Bookkeeping looks at who keeps track of it, and the one on Sharing the Wealth addresses giving some of it back. But perhaps the question that causes the most conflict is Who decides how to spend it and save it? You need to address this head on. It's not going to go away, and it's going to recur as an issue throughout your married life, particularly as your income and needs change.

As in so many other areas, marriages seem to attract one of each, a spender and a saver. It must be some sort of cosmic law! In fact, it's probably good for your marriage to have a level of tension in this area, a pulling in two different directions. Otherwise, you'd both end up either spending more than you could afford or becoming extremist tightwads.

One good way to approach this "problem" is to reword the original ques-tion: How do *we* decide how much to spend and how much to save? You both need to be equally involved regardless of who is the primary breadwinner. The chapters on making small and large decisions are a good starting place. Who's good at it?

Second, revisit the question you previously encountered in the chapter "Breadwinning": What does money mean to me? Ask your wife what it means to her. Write down both your answers without comment or judgment. Money might mean security or success. It could be a means to an end or a challenge unto itself. It's also likely to involve your desire to nurture her as well as her desire to be independent. And more. Note whether your attitudes reflect or oppose those of your parents. Remember that you get to choose your own perspective; you don't have to keep their viewpoints if they don't serve you. Your circumstances may be different.

In *The First Year of Marriage*, Miriam Arnold and Samuel Paulker conclude: "It is easier to quarrel about money than about other, deeper, more sensitive topics. Most people feel less threatened by pointing to money as a problem than by speaking about an absence of trust or a feeling of nurturance in their love relationship." Once you begin to get a handle on what money means to you, it may be easier to deal with those issues head on; otherwise, they may come up subtly each time you guys buy something.

Third, decide what part money plays in your joint vision. (See Appendix: Joint Vision Statement.) How will money help you achieve your goals and aspirations? The very dynamics of your money discussions will help you shape this vision.

One of the main reasons for having a long-term vision is to guide you in deciding whether to buy a new car or put money away for your child's education. Find the mix that serves you both. The spending-saving debate doesn't have to be marriage-threatening or even that big a deal. You guys are in this together, so go at it together. Move toward her and encourage her to move toward you.

A husband balances saving and spending money, and he feels good about it.

46

Supporting

Stand by your woman.

Tammy Wynette (paraphrased)

Support usually congers up notions of money, and certainly everyone's marriage needs financial support for subsistence. But the other definition of support—the subtler one—is the more important to your marriage in the long haul. Meaningful support involves courage, faith, and confidence; it means comforting your wife and giving her moral encouragement. It calls for sustaining her at the deepest levels.

Supporting your wife in no way implies total agreement with her every thought and action. Nowhere does it preclude independent thinking or behavior for either of you. You are still free to grow in your own direction, to take on your own challenges.

Women have been full-fledged partners in the work force for a while, now. Inequities may keep their salaries lower on the average, but no one can disagree that women are as capable of independent living as men. Yet they still marry us. And choose interdependence with us. It has to do with love and support. It has to do with empowerment: providing a secure base so she can make full use of her powers.

If she has a conflict with someone at work or elsewhere, supporting her doesn't necessarily mean taking her side. But it does mean *not* siding against her, and may mean reminding her that she has the skills she needs to resolve the problem.

Your wife may pursue career goals that strain your marriage. Her friends or politics or religion or causes may demand time away from you. She may be traveling life's path at a pace different from yours. None of this prevents your full support. You are supporting her growth and honoring her choices.

Ask her how things are going, what she's decided to do about a situation she mentioned a while ago, if there's anything you can do to help. Show your interest in your words and your body language, and take care not to judge her independent thought. Individuality is not a threat to your marriage.

As an independent, thinking man of action, you are seeking your own self-empowerment whether you know it or not. You want to attain your goals, succeed in your career, stay in shape, be happy, find peace in your life—a whole bunch of things. Sometimes it seems life conspires against those aspirations, so you especially appreciate it when your wife supports you. When she bolsters you and stands by you, she is helping you empower yourself to achieve your dreams. She deserves the same from you.

A husband supports his wife.

47

Taking a Closer Look

If you've poked around this book some, you've probably seen the repeated message that you should look beneath the surface. What's the big deal? Can't things just be simple?

Sure. If your wife is late picking you up, you may be perturbed only because you're cold and wet—and therefore there's no deeper truth to be uncovered. But whenever she *really* gets to you, *really* pisses you off, take a closer look. You'll find that you are rarely upset for the reason you think. There's often a deeper reason under the obvious one, and it may help to acknowledge it.

Michael complains to Pam because she has a way of putting things off until the last minute. As an organized and self-disciplined person, he says her haphazard ways drive him nuts. How can she live that way? Today he blew up because she had to race to the bank before it closed, even though he had reminded her this morning. What is wrong with her, anyway? he keeps asking.

Pam's latest last-minute check cashing may have triggered Michael's outburst, but take a closer look. It could be Michael is saying *She never listens to me,* (which could really mean *She doesn't obey me*). It could be *Why doesn't she hold organization in the same high regard that I do?* (which means *Why isn't she more like me?*) In other words, something else is going on; otherwise his reactions would be less dramatic.

Unless Michael loves feeling upset, he wants to get out of the bad mood as soon as possible. Admitting the deeper reason is a good way to deal with anger, and thus get past it.

You are carrying a heavy box into the house. Your wife, walking ahead of you, unlocks the door but fails to hold it open. It slams shut. You call her back.

She holds it open as you struggle past but she doesn't acknowledge her "guilt." You tilt your head sardonically, shooting her "that look."

Do you get steamed, or do you figure she was just being spacey? Choosing the latter is better for your health, but if you choose anger, take a closer look. It may be a gnawing feeling of powerlessness. *I can't make her see and do things my way. I can't control her.* Or a need for a dose of righteousness. *She's inconsiderate. I would have held the door for her. I'd have been more thoughtful.* Or even more deeply, it may be a sense that she doesn't love you enough. Acknowledging a deeper issue helps you resolve it and saves a lot of wear and tear.

On the other side of the coin, a husband recognizes that his wife will occasionally hit the ceiling for reasons buried in the basement. That you didn't bring her a cup of coffee when you poured one for yourself may not be the main reason she just snapped at you.

- Was her job particularly trying today? Is it unsatisfying?
- Have unresolved issues with her parents, siblings, or old friends been brewing?
- Have you been ignoring her lately?
- Does she have a sense that you don't love her enough?

There are dozens of reasons why people get upset and angry. The most recent "event" is usually the one we focus on. It doesn't hurt to take a closer look. Ask yourself, *What am I (or what is she) really angry about? Is there anything else going on?*

A husband is not afraid to take a closer look.

48

Taking Offense

Don't do it.

A tall order for many husbands, but think of it this way: How are you going to be a strong, responsible man of action if you get insulted by what she says or does? Or *doesn't* say or do?

> *You missed a spot.*
> *You did it again.*
> *Are you going to leave that on the floor?*
> *Is that it?*
> *(Sighs, eye rolling, lip pursing, sarcasm, antagonistic humor.)*

Is your reaction to any of the above one of feeling put down or insulted? Will you take umbrage? If so, what comes next? Escalation to a fight, turning away from her, feeling angry and hurt, replaying the tape of what happened, thinking of ways to get back at her? If you were in control of yourself, you'd surely never choose these negative reactions. Here's a truth to help you reassume that control:

> *I choose my responses to life; it's part of my strength as a husband and a man. If someone judges me (even if insult was intended, as it rarely is), I may feel momentarily stung, but then I get to choose how to respond and how to feel about it.*

If you follow Rule 3, you will take responsibility for your own happiness. The hardest part is recognizing that you have the power to choose your

117

response. In other words, you have the ability to respond any way you choose; you have response-ability.

Once you accept personal responsibility, the rest of the process is alot easier. Who wouldn't rather enjoy making love or dancing or snuggling on the couch in front of your favorite TV show than picking the scab off an old hurt? That's what feeling offended is about—keeping the hurt active, choosing pain.

One of the best ways to move beyond pain is to lighten the moment. Parents know that humor and lightness are necessary for dealing with their children. Kids throw tantrums, disobey, and get overwhelmed by pubescent hormones. Sometimes just distracting their attention with something silly can change the mood. Grownups sometime get out of balance, too, and those times call for the same even temper and gentleness. Use your ability to lighten the moment the next time you begin to feel offended.

- *No, as a matter of fact I'm not being a wimp; it's just that I forgot to eat my spinach before I talked to the tax auditor. Now, let's work together on this. What can we do next?*
- *Ooh, that smarts! I'm sorry you feel that way. I didn't forget to cancel the paper on purpose. Tell me what would help make things right.*
- *You're right; maybe I have been neglecting you. And I'd like to make it up to you. Call the florist!*

Though a wife certainly knows her husband's vulnerable points, chances are that she rarely intends consciously to hurt you. If you do feel genuinely offended, find out if she meant to insult you. If not, it was a matter of poor communication. If so, ask why. Was her pain so great that she wanted to inflict some on you? What was her pain?

This "action" approach gets you off the downwardly spiraling anguish of feeling offended. It puts you on the upwardly soaring path of problem solving. Tackle your hurts; don't wallow in the misery they bring. Don't choose pain.

A husband has dominion over himself.

49

Trying New Things
or
Dealing with differences

Her: *Here, try this. It's great.*
You: *What's in it?*
Her: *Just try it.*
You: *Well, I like to know what's in something before I eat it.*
Her: *Come on. Be surprised for once. Don't you trust me? I wouldn't poison you, you know.*
You: *That's not the point.*

What's going on here? This conversation could continue for a few more minutes, until someone gets angry and walks off. Or until she relents and tells the ingredients. Or you reluctantly try the dish without knowing the contents. Sometimes one of you gives in but doesn't feel good about it.

You're arguing about food and taste, or about trusting your spouse's judgment, right?

Wrong.

You're now arguing about SOMETHING ELSE.

You're arguing about your differences. The two of you experiment in life differently, and now you're in a snit over it. It's probably not the first time. It may not even be about food. Clothes, hair style, where to go on vacation—any area where experimentation is key.

What a waste. But what a good lesson, too—an excellent example of how we can learn from our differences. Here's how:

119

Start by accepting reality. The fact is that you're one way; she's another. You analyze, she leaps in. You're careful; she's adventurous. It fills her sense of wonder to experiment with new tastes. You're more wary. You've been taught to mistrust, to look below the surface. You've been stung a few times, and you're not going to let it happen again. These differences are parts of your respective characters. Neither of you is *right* or *wrong*. You're just who you are. She's just who she is.

Sometimes, one of you will try to "prove" the other wrong by showing the logic of the argument. Your way doesn't make sense, you argue; mine does. You shake your head wondering how she can think that way.

Understand this: She is not "careless and rash"; she's different. If you label her with value words, you're making her wrong; you're judging her. (Of course, the same goes for you. You are not "stodgy and stuck in the mud." Labels make you wrong, too.) Remember, too that her experiments—even her daring—are not meant to challenge or disturb you. She just doesn't mind a few misses or failures. Even superstar baseball players succeed only one out of every three times they bat.

Let's look at the opposite scenario for a moment: You're the one who always wants to try daring new adventures, both big and little. She's more cautious. She researches a product for weeks before deciding, whereas you tend to impulse buying. You're likely to drive down a road just to see where it goes; she needs a map.

The same logic applies. Think about it. She's okay. Just because she likes to analyze, doesn't mean she's closed herself off to life. It just means she's a bit more wary than you. Be easy with her. She either inherited the trait or learned it. Either way, it's part of her. Put yourself in her shoes. There's a little fear of the unknown in all of us. Including you. Hers is more pronounced, perhaps, but it's the same fear that all our ancestors felt through times of cold and dark and hardship. For many people, it's not an easy state to get past.

Rule 2 reminds us not to judge or label her behavior. Making another person wrong makes you right, and all that gets you is the booby prize. All you manage to do is upset her and fool yourself into thinking the issue is resolved.

Another good reason for avoiding labels is they get you off track. You're now arguing about name calling and how it hurts somebody's feelings. Stay on track.

Ask her to meet you half way. One time try it her way and do it whole-heartedly. Later tell her what the experience was like for you. Ask her to do the counterpart. One time she's to do it your way enthusiastically. Thank her for her efforts.

Try this in a lot of areas. She wants to see a new movie or try a new neighborhood restaurant without knowing anything about it. You want to read several reviews before going. What areas for compromise are there? Remember your goal of moving toward each other.

A husband deals with differences by honoring them.

50

Walking the Perimeter

Think of your immediate family as a circle or, perhaps better, a sphere. You guys are in the center. The outside rim is the edge between you and the rest of the world. That border needs to be tended.

Tend it physically, emotionally, mentally, and spiritually. Take turns. You're both adults, both equally responsible for your family.

You've both got strengths, and those strengths are probably different. One of you is better at keeping track of goings-on in the neighborhood for example. That one should walk those perimeters: chat with neighbors, keep up on zoning plans, sense trends in the community—whatever it takes to know what's out there.

Your home has a perimeter, too. Walls, yards, fences, streams—all these form physical boundaries for your family circle, and they have to be tended as well. If she's better at this than you, she should have the job; if not, it's yours.

Think about all the ways you interact with the world outside your circle— emergency phone numbers, fire escape routes, utility maintenance and repair— even newspaper and mail delivery. Someone needs to be charged with responsibility for these.

Someone also needs to be charged with the overall security of your circle. Historically, this has been the husband's job, and in most it families remains so. If you're lucky, the need to patrol is slight. Whatever degree of vigilance against peril to your family is needed, don't ignore it. Between the two of you, assign this task to the one most suited physically and psychologically. In most cases, it'll be you.

Sometimes, one of you needs to take some time out. When this happens, the other's task is to walk the perimeter to creat a safe place. Hold her calls. Tell friends she's "on retreat."

Accept this necessary job and do it well. But don't read more into it than is there. Being the perimeter walker doesn't suggest authority over other family members. Nor does it imply physical superiority or use of force. Most times, planning ahead for eventualities and offering a gentle first response will work much better than any kind of aggressive stance. What you are doing is setting boundaries and deciding how permeable they should be—an extension of your most basic responsibility to your family. Letting down the drawbridge can be the best part of the job.

A husband is aware of his family's perimeters and walks them proudly.

Appendix

Joint Vision Statement

Many couples find it helpful to work on their statements separately at first, and then to meld them. You should both fully agree on the final product. A helpful way to proceed is to divide your Joint Vision Statement into categories and to start each goal in that section with a strong verb.

Some sample categories (with sample goals):

Material: to create and maintain a home where our friends and family feel comfortable and welcome
Emotional: to feel free to express ourselves honestly
Intellectual: to support each other in continuing our educations
Spiritual: to live the principles we believe (Specify them)

Create your own categories and your own goals. Even if you don't actually write them down, talk about them with her. Review and update them at least yearly; your anniversary is a perfect time. The payoff is to provide a general guide for your life and to help you in the ongoing creation of your role as Husband. Knowing your goals will go a long way toward helping you figure out that role. This marriage is your creation. There is no other one like it.

Create your role as Husband according to the dreams and values you and your wife share.

Acknowledgments

Our deep thanks go to many people for helping bring this project to fruition.

For inspiration and understanding in our own marriage, Bruce and Sheila Barth whose counseling helped us form our vision and whose ideas have deeply influenced our own.

For the commitment, Andy's small group: Jim Ashmen, Jim Goluch, Kristine Gregos, Peter Lewiss, Linda Meidlinger, Patti Provence, Donna Smith, Dan Spar, and Tiffany Vanderhoof.

For editorial input and review and for encouragement and love: Bill & Gina Cressey, Tina Flynn and Tom Bush, Ralph Hoar and Russ Francisco, Bill and Laurie Jasien, John & Lyn Kilday, Steve Leisge and Liz Darby, Pat & Dan McCarthy, Diane Merchant and Scott Loomis, Jennifer Messersmith, Peggy Meyer, Heather Murphy, Mary Ruwart, and Pam & Michael Wright.

For healthy hearts: Benjamin Aaron, Karen Lawson, and Dean Ornish.

Teresa Murphy and Andrew Murphy

Teri & Andy Murphy have each had wide-ranging careers with a central focus on communications with an avocation of personal growth.

Andy has written 37 text books, most for students of English as a foreign language, and has lectured widely in areas of personal growth, such as negotiating, listening, assertive communications, and confidence. He taught high school in his native Philadelphia and later directed language schools in Peru, Mexico, and Washington, D.C. He currently designs and teaches public speaking and writing classes for government and industry in the Washington, D.C. area.

Teri, who now writes and gives seminars for corporate and government clients in various aspects of communications skills, graduated from the University of California at Berkeley with a degree in Communications and Public Policy. She worked as a writer, editor, speech writer, and policy analyst for three federal agencies in Washington D.C. before becoming an independent consultant in business communications.

The Murphys met via a personal ad Teri ran in *Washingtonian Magazine* that was designed to identify her perfect mate. "It was more successful than either of us could have imagined," Andy says. "We had similar, ideal images of the roles marriage mates play—not only in the theater of life but also in aiding each other's growth as individuals. Our marriage has been a laboratory for testing those ideas. What we've discovered, much to our delight, is that all this stuff we believe about husbands (and wives) is valid. It works!"

If you enjoyed *The Husband's Manual*, share it with someone getting married—or already married.

Quantity	Price per book
1	$9.00
2-4	$7.20
over 4	$5.40

- -

Order Form:

Name _____

Address _____

_____

Number of books_____ x Price per book _____ = _____

Virginia residents add 4% sales tax _____

Shipping ___*$2.00*___

Total _____

Remit to
Cherrydale Books Box 10329 Arlington, VA 22210